THE ENTREPRENEUR'S GUIDE TO WRITING A WINNING BUSINESS PLAN

A STEP-BY-STEP BEGINNER'S GUIDE FROM IDEA TO SUCCESS TO RAISE CAPITAL AND ACHIEVE PROFITABILITY

KAY CARROLL

© **Copyright 2023 - All rights reserved.**

The content contained within this book may not be reproduced, duplicated or transmitted without direct written permission from the author or the publisher.

Under no circumstances will any blame or legal responsibility be held against the publisher, or author, for any damages, reparation, or monetary loss due to the information contained within this book, either directly or indirectly.

Legal Notice:

This book is copyright protected. It is only for personal use. You cannot amend, distribute, sell, use, quote or paraphrase any part, or the content within this book, without the consent of the author or publisher.

Disclaimer Notice:

Please note the information contained within this document is for educational and entertainment purposes only. All effort has been executed to present accurate, up to date, reliable, complete information. No warranties of any kind are declared or implied. Readers acknowledge that the author is not engaged in the rendering of legal, financial, medical or professional advice. The content within this book has been derived from various sources. Please consult a licensed professional before attempting any techniques outlined in this book.

By reading this document, the reader agrees that under no circumstances is the author responsible for any losses, direct or indirect, that are incurred as a result of the use of the information contained within this document, including, but not limited to, errors, omissions, or inaccuracies.

CONTENTS

Introduction   5

1. What are the key elements of a business plan?   11
2. How to write a solid executive summary   27
3. How to nail your company description   37
4. Showcasing your expertise with an industry analysis   51
5. Putting together a solid market analysis   69
6. Demonstrating your knowledge of the space with a competitive analysis   81
7. Building a sales and marketing plan to beat your competition   91
8. Describing the service or product that you are offering   109
9. Writing an operational plan to guide your business   123
10. Building a financial plan that will allow your business to succeed   139

Conclusion   175
References   181

INTRODUCTION

After over twenty-five years of starting, operating, and selling businesses, I've been fortunate to learn firsthand, through a lot of trial and error, the importance of having a solid plan in place when starting or growing a business. I have stories of my lack of competitive research coming back to haunt me in the form of an established, well-known software business entering the same submarket that I intended to target. I have other stories where my relentless pursuit of preparation was the very reason I edged out the competition to win a particular client.

Fortunately, my experience spans many disciplines, including short-term rentals, long-term rentals, high-tech software companies, a publishing business, and even a chain of ice cream stores! From this, I've learned all the ways to set yourself up for success with your company and, arguably more importantly, all the major mistakes to avoid.

This book is a culmination of all those experiences meant to give you a head start on building your business.

Your business begins and ends with your business plan. We will discuss in-depth throughout this book how your business plan is more than just a way to raise capital from investors or secure a loan from a bank. Your business plan must be a living, breathing document that you use to evaluate the viability of your business and ensure that you're guiding your company down the right path as you scale.

Each chapter of this book goes through the different sections that should be included in your business plan. The process of building your business plan will be eye-opening in that you will put your business under a microscope, dissecting its viability each step of the way.

At the end of this process, you will truly understand what your business does, how your business does that thing, and where you fit in the overall ecosystem. Knowledge of these areas is essential to the success of your business and will allow you to build a profitable, sustainable business.

It has been said that "ignoring competition is like playing with your eyes closed; you may think you're winning, but you're actually losing sight of the bigger picture."

Read that one more time and let it sink in.

You will only succeed in this endeavor by entering your business's start-up phase with your eyes wide open. And if you are already operating a business, you must open your eyes to the reality in which you operate. Unfortunately, you cannot afford to ignore reality.

Through reading this book and following the steps to create your business plan, you will hopefully learn that a well-written business plan serves as a roadmap for success. A business plan helps you to define your goals, deeply understand your target market, build strategies for reaching that target market, and ultimately achieve your goals.

A business plan is a vital tool that can help you secure funding, attract and retain customers, and stay on track as you work to achieve your vision. In this book, I'll share my experience and expertise on how to write a comprehensive, effective, and compelling business plan. Whether you are starting a new venture or looking to grow an existing one, this guide will provide you with the information, tools, and guidance you need to create a winning plan.

As you read, you will notice a few overarching themes throughout your business plan's different sections. For the sake of emphasis, I do hit on those themes multiple times, and for the sake of clarity, here are the main points of focus for every section of your business plan:

1. The ultimate purpose of a business plan is to lay out your business goals and, in painstaking detail, show how you will achieve these goals. As such, you must prepare clear, concise descriptions of what you are trying to do and how you will accomplish it. You also need to ensure that it is simple for someone unfamiliar with your business to understand.
2. You are the expert of your business, and it is your job to prove to the readers of your business plan that you are such. To that end, each section of your business plan must be thoroughly researched and include all relevant details to prove that your outlook of the market and your approach to capitalizing on that outlook are correct.
3. Be honest about the challenges in your business and about potential competitors. It is your job to paint a picture for potential investors,

lenders, and yourself that there is a market opportunity. However, ignoring competition or downplaying significant challenges will not result in the outcome that you want, so be honest about the risks and put forth ways to mitigate those risks.

Before you embark on this journey, remember that the process of writing this business plan is long, but it is essential. Take your time to think through each section of the business plan.

Each section, more or less, correlates to a department within your business and will ultimately dictate the success of your business.

Take this time to refine your approach to everything from the product or service you provide to how you are marketing that product or service to your potential customers. The more time that you spend on your plan, within reason, of course, the better prepared you will be to start and run your business.

1

WHAT ARE THE KEY ELEMENTS OF A BUSINESS PLAN?

If approached correctly, your business plan will guide you through the steps of validating whether or not your idea is a viable business. While it feels cumbersome to go through the paces of each section, the result of this exercise will be a well-thought-out plan with which you are intimately familiar. Undoubtedly, you will be the expert on your business, which will pay off when it comes time to pitch investors and grow your business.

In the most basic of definitions, a business plan is a document that outlines the strategy and operations of a company and is typically used to secure funding or to guide the growth of the business. In reality, a business plan is your hypothesis of how you intend to approach a gap in the market and what you expect the outcome to be. Whether you are creating a "never done before" software company or opening a laundromat, you have a goal in mind for what your business can accomplish, and your business plan will flesh out the details of how you will achieve this goal.

A typical business plan will include several key elements. We will outline these elements here, then each chapter of this book will go into detail about what should be included in each section. I will also address some common themes that will span all of the sections of your business plan as well as mistakes to avoid and ways to help your business plan stand out from the rest.

At a high level, your business plan will include the following sections: an executive summary, a company description, an industry analysis, a market analysis, a competitive analysis, a sales and marketing plan, a description of your service or product line, an operational plan, a financial plan, and an appendix section. In addition, we briefly review the contents and goals of each section here before going into more detail in each chapter of this book.

EXECUTIVE SUMMARY

The executive summary portion of a business plan provides a brief overview of the entire business plan and is the first thing that potential investors and lenders will read. It should include a summary of the most important information about your business, such as your value proposition, target market, and financial projections.

If your business plan was a movie, you could view the executive summary as the movie trailer. This may be the only section of your business plan that an investor reads, and only if you are able to pique her interest will she continue through the remainder of your brilliant plan.

Be brief, but aim to dazzle.

COMPANY DESCRIPTION

The company description section provides a detailed description of your company, including its history, ownership structure, and any relevant background information. It should also include a mission statement that clearly communicates your company's goals and objectives.

This section will be relatively robust if your company has been in business and has a history. However, if you're putting a business plan together for a new company, the relevant information here will include research and your hypothesis rather than history.

Either way, this is your place to begin setting yourself up as the expert who can tackle the business opportunity at hand.

INDUSTRY ANALYSIS:

The industry analysis section provides an overview of the industry in which your company operates, including market size, growth rate, trends, and major competitors. It should also include a SWOT analysis highlighting your company's strengths, weaknesses, opportunities, and threats.

You'll find that a common theme throughout your business plan is positioning yourself as an expert. The industry analysis section is the ideal place to position yourself as such. You need to be not only an expert in operating your business but also an expert in the industry in which you're operating.

For this section and many of the following areas of your business plan, you are only as good as your research on the topic. Therefore, ensuring that your industry analysis is well-researched will be crucial to your success.

MARKET ANALYSIS:

This market analysis section provides an overview of the target market for your company's products or services, including market size, growth rate, trends, and major segments. It should also include information on your company's target customers, including demographic and psychographic information.

Again, the market analysis portion of your business plan must be based on extensive research that you have done on the topic. Spend the time doing the pre-work to achieve the results that you want.

COMPETITIVE ANALYSIS:

This competitive analysis section provides an overview of your company's major competitors, including their strengths and weaknesses. It should also include information on your company's competitive advantage, such as its unique selling proposition.

No investor or lender expects that you will not have competition in your business. In fact, if you claim to have no competition, then investors will think one of two things: either you have not done your homework, and you are therefore not thorough in your approach, or if there is no competition, then they will question whether this is a market in which they should invest. Regardless of what conclusion investors come to, the result of this kind of investor speculation is the same: they will not invest in your business.

We'll cover everything you need to know to analyze your competition later in this book properly.

SALES AND MARKETING PLAN:

Your business plan's sales and marketing section provides a detailed description of the company's sales and marketing strategy, including how it plans to reach and acquire customers. It should also include information on your company's pricing strategy and any promotions or advertising plans.

You might have the most novel, innovative offering out there, but if you cannot demonstrate your ability to bring customers "through the door," then your business will not be successful. Your sales and marketing strategy is the backbone of your ability to generate revenue and is another critical piece of your business plan.

SERVICE OR PRODUCT LINE:

This section describes the company's products or services, including their features, benefits, and pricing. If you offer a physical product, this section should also include information on the company's production processes, location, and equipment.

Depending on your business, you must detail what you offer your customers. It is also wise to demonstrate that you have deep knowledge of who your customers are in your sales and marketing plan and your description of your service or product line. In addition, your service or products are offered in order to meet the needs of a specific set of customers, and it is imperative to know who those customers are.

OPERATIONAL PLAN:

This section provides a detailed description of the company's operations, including information on the company's management and organizational structure, as well as any relevant logistics and supply chain information.

The operational plan is near and dear to my heart. I've always been an operator and thrive on figuring out how to bring a particular initiative to fruition. As such, this section of the book might have some extra flair.

Like the many sections before, the operational plan will be specific to the type of business you are running or intend to run; however, the basic structure is the same. And the purpose of this section is to demonstrate to the reader that you know what needs to be done to build a successful business and how to get it done.

FINANCIAL PLAN:

This section describes the company's financial projections, including projected income statements, balance sheets, and cash flow statements. It should also include information on the company's funding requirements and short- and long-term financial goals.

At the core of any business is the financial plan. We can all dream of big things for our newly formed entities, but if the numbers behind the business don't make sense, then there's no reason to pursue the business further.

Meaning if there is no line of site to profit with acceptable profit margins, then you should quit. Harsh but true, and taking this kind of approach to your business will save you a lot of time and money.

APPENDICES:

This section includes supporting documents such as resumes of key personnel, legal documents, market research, financial data, and industry information.

Many of the documents in the appendix are things you will need when you get to the capital raise or loan due diligence phase. While there is a somewhat standard set of documents that you can prepare, the final set of documents will depend on the investors or lenders to whom you are speaking.

I can remember in a series A round of funding for one of my software businesses, we were asked to produce every contract that we had ever signed, but in a later (and larger) round, the lead investor had no interest in every minute detail. The due diligence requirements vary from investor to investor, so it will behoove you to keep the many analyses and documents you have put together in the appendix of your business plan.

It is worth noting that this is just a general outline, and the specific elements and content of your business plan will depend on the type of business you are starting and the needs of your target audience.

For example, a software company might include product screenshots, prototypes, and mock-ups in its business plan. Alternatively, a daycare facility for dogs might need to produce the marketing materials used to drive customer acquisition (complete with adorable puppy photos, of course).

As such, when writing your business plan, it is essential to be as detailed and specific as possible. Provide concrete examples and data to support your claims that are specific to your business, and make sure that all of the information is accurate and up-to-date.

It is also crucial to keep in mind that a business plan is a living document that should be reviewed and updated regularly as your business grows and evolves. It should be used to guide the company's strategy and not just as a document created to secure funding. By treating this as an evolving document, you will be well-positioned to grow your business and bring on additional capital at any moment.

While this process might seem overwhelming, we will break down each section of your business plan throughout the course of this book. In each section, we will also review the common mistakes people make when it comes to their business plans and the key elements to make your business plan stand out from the rest.

Now, here are the biggest mistakes people make when writing a business plan. Not to worry, we will spend the remaining chapters of this book ensuring you avoid these mistakes as you write your business plan.

LACK OF MARKET RESEARCH:

One of the biggest mistakes people make when writing a business plan is not conducting sufficient market research. A thorough understanding of the industry and target market is essential to create a realistic and effective business plan.

Doing your research is a common theme throughout this book. You need to be the expert in all aspects of your business, and it is your job to demonstrate this expertise to any investors or lenders with whom you are speaking. These individuals are trusting you with their money, and it is your job to deliver the return that you are projecting. Those funding your business need to trust that you will either multiply their investment or pay back the loan they are giving you. To be comfortable parting with their money, they need to trust that you are indeed an expert.

NOT INCLUDING FINANCIAL PROJECTIONS:

Another common mistake is not including detailed financial projections, such as projected income statements, balance sheets, and cash flow statements. These are important for demonstrating the business's financial viability and can be crucial in securing funding or investments.

These are also the projections that will allow investors to "do the math" on whether or not you will provide them with a return on investment. Not including these statements does not mean that investors will take your word for the fact that the business will make eventually become profitable. In fact, the lack of financial projections will cause investors to walk away.

NOT TAILORING THE PLAN TO THE AUDIENCE

A business plan should be tailored to the specific audience reading the plan, whether that be investors, lenders, or potential customers. Neglecting this aspect can make your business plan less effective and less likely to achieve its intended purpose. As you go through the process of establishing and raising funds for your business, you may need to create multiple versions of your business plan that are ever so slightly different from one another.

When you walk into a room with investors or lenders, you have some idea of who they are and what their investment thesis is. You must use this to your advantage when crafting the business plan you present to each audience.

For example, if you know that a particular lender is interested in the payback period for their loan, be sure to highlight the projected payback period in your executive summary and provide details behind this specific figure in the financial projection section of your business plan.

LACK OF SPECIFICITY:

Your business plan should be as specific as possible. Avoid using overly general language and ensure the information included is accurate and up-to-date. Being clear and concrete in the plan will make it more convincing and easier to understand.

The underlying theme with a majority of the mistakes that people typically make when writing a business plan is a lack of research. A lack of specificity in your plan is rooted in a lack of research. The good news is that this is entirely within your control to correct.

NOT HAVING A CLEAR VALUE PROPOSITION:

A value proposition is a statement describing how your business solves a problem or fulfills your target customer's needs. A business plan without a clear value proposition can make it difficult for investors to understand the value of the business.

Further, distilling that value proposition in a way that is easy to digest is a key part of your business plan and your approach to winning customers for your business.

NOT HIGHLIGHTING COMPETITIVE ADVANTAGE:

A business plan should clearly explain what makes your business unique and how it stands out from the competition. Without this information, it can be difficult for investors to understand why the business is a good investment opportunity.

Think of a competitive advantage as building a moat around your business. You want to dig a deep, wide moat to keep others out of your market, and it will take deliberate action on your part to not only identify your competitive advantage but also to demonstrate it to potential investors.

NOT INCLUDING A CLEAR CALL TO ACTION:

A business plan should include a clear call to action that tells the reader what you want them to do next, whether it be to review the rest of the plan, contact you to discuss investment opportunities, or something else.

You are not walking into the room with investors or lenders just to chat. Your goal is to walk into the room with your business plan and walk out of the room with capital secured to start growing your business. If you don't make that clear to the individuals you're speaking with, then you will not accomplish your goal.

IGNORING THE IMPORTANCE OF DESIGN AND FORMATTING:

A business plan should be visually appealing and easy to read. Poor design and formatting can make it less likely that investors will take the time to read it.

There is a reason that the most successful companies worldwide have large marketing budgets - visuals matter. Many resources are out there to help you design and make your business plan visually appealing. Fiverr, for example, is a great resource for finding freelance design help. Freelancers on this platform can bring your business plan to life with stunning visuals.

NOT REVIEWING AND UPDATING THE PLAN REGULARLY:

A business plan is a living document that should be reviewed and updated regularly as the business grows and evolves. Neglecting to do so can make it less effective as a tool for guiding the company's strategy and raising capital.

When utilized correctly, your business plan will guide how you build and grow your business. Continuing to iterate on this plan with each day of learning will pay you back tenfold as you build your business.

2

HOW TO WRITE A SOLID EXECUTIVE SUMMARY

s discussed in the previous chapter, the executive summary is akin to a movie trailer.

Done well, the executive summary of your business plan will draw readers in. If done poorly, the executive summary will be the only portion of your business plan that someone reads. In this chapter, we'll discuss how to fall into the category of "done well" and help you avoid the most common mistakes people make.

Because the executive summary is the first thing that potential investors and lenders will read, you must take the time to write a clear and compelling executive summary that effectively communicates the essential information about your business. The executive summary will either hook your reader or cause them to pass on the opportunity you are presenting.

A SOLID EXECUTIVE SUMMARY SHOULD INCLUDE THE FOLLOWING KEY ELEMENTS.

A brief description of your business:

The description of your business should include your company's name, what it does, and what products or services it offers. You should also include your mission statement to define the purpose and goals of your business. For example, if someone were to stop you on the street and ask you what your company does, the brief description section in your executive summary should be your answer to that question.

The problem your business solves:

Explain the problem or need in the market your business aims to solve. This problem might be an issue that your target customer is facing or a current gap in the market that you intend to take advantage of.

Anyone interested in investing in your business will need to understand the basics of the problem you are solving. You will also want to paint a compelling picture of why solving this problem for your potential customers is important.

Your solution:

Clearly describe how your products or service solve the problem you've identified.

This section of your business plan is your opportunity to bring your brilliant solution to light. You'll go into more detail later in your business plan; however, this is one of the first opportunities for you to explain to the reader how your solution is tailored to the problem that you just described.

Your target market:

Identify your target customer, the target market size, and the growth opportunities for your business. Understanding your customers, the market size, and the potential size of your business is arguably one of the most important parts of the research behind your business plan.

You might have an outstanding solution to a problem out there, but if there are only two people who can use your product or service, then it is not likely that your business can be large enough to survive. But, of course, if those two customers pay you millions of dollars each year, then that is a different story!

Your competitive advantage:

Explain what makes your business unique and how it will stand out. As discussed in the previous chapter, your competitive advantage is like a moat you build around your business. Anyone reading your business plan will want to understand what it is that you do that others cannot do.

In this way, you've built a competitive advantage over other companies in the market.

Financial Projections:

Include a high-level overview of your financial projections, such as revenue, profitability, and funding requirements. We'll dive deeper into this topic later in the book; however, having financial projections early in your business plan is a great way to signal to the individuals reading your business plan that you have thought through each detail, including how you will pay back any loans that you are looking to secure.

The Ask:

Explain what you are asking for from the reader, whether it be funding, partnership, or any other specific request. Going into a particular meeting, it might not be clear what the purpose of the meeting is.

Be sure to include in the executive summary precisely what you hope to walk away from each meeting with.

As mentioned previously, tailoring your business plan to each audience, including what you are asking of each audience, is key to your success.

AS WE CONTINUE TO SET YOU UP FOR SUCCESS, WE WILL NOW JUMP INTO THE TOP MISTAKES PEOPLE MAKE WHEN WRITING AN EXECUTIVE SUMMARY FOR A BUSINESS PLAN.

Not including a clear and compelling value proposition:

One of the most common mistakes people make when writing an executive summary is not including a clear and compelling value proposition. A value proposition is a statement describing how your business solves a problem or fulfills your target customer's needs. It's essential to include this information in your executive summary so that potential investors and lenders understand the value of your business.

Being too generic:

Another mistake people often make when writing an executive summary is being too generic. A generic executive summary will not stand out and might not be remembered by the reader, which can be costly. Instead, focus on what makes your business unique and how it stands out from the competition. Doing this upfront in your executive summary will help you to differentiate yourself and your business.

Not including financial projections:

Including financial projections in your executive summary is important, as it gives investors and lenders an idea of your company's financial potential. Without financial projections, your executive summary may lack credibility, and potential investors and lenders may be less likely to consider your business plan.

Further, if you intend to ask the reader of your business plan for an investment, they will need to have some idea of how your business will become profitable to consider investing.

Focusing too much on the past:

Some executive summaries focus too much on the past, such as the company's history or its founders. While this information can be helpful, it is important to remember that your executive summary's main focus should be on your business's future potential.

Neglecting to tailor the summary to the target audience:

An executive summary should be tailored to the specific audience for which it is written. For example, suppose you are writing a business plan to attract investors. In that case, you'll want to focus on the potential for financial return, while if you're writing a plan for a bank loan, you'll want to focus on the company's creditworthiness and ability to repay the loan. By neglecting this aspect, readers may lose interest in your business plan before getting past the executive summary.

AND HERE ARE THE BIG THINGS YOU CAN DO TO MAKE YOUR EXECUTIVE SUMMARY STAND OUT FROM THE REST.

Make it clear and concise:

Your executive summary should be brief and to the point. Avoid using overly technical language or jargon, and make sure that the most important information is easy to find. Use language that would be simple for a fifth-grader to understand. It seems counterintuitive; however, the ability to explain a problem clearly and concisely is a highly coveted business skill and is very important when you are briefing individuals who are new to the subject matter.

Highlight the problem your business solves:

Clearly describe the problem or need in the market your business aims to solve and explain how your products or services solve it. By highlighting the acute problem your business solves, potential investors and lenders will better understand the value of your business.

Show your competitive advantage:

Explain what makes your business unique and how it stands out from the competition. Explaining this will help your executive summary stand out, demonstrating why your business is a good investment opportunity.

Use storytelling and imagination :

Instead of simply listing facts and figures, try to use storytelling techniques to capture the reader's attention and imagination. Storytelling can make your executive summary more engaging and memorable, which will help it stand out from other business plans that your readers might be reviewing.

Include a clear call to action:

At the end of your executive summary, include a clear call to action that tells the reader what you want them to do next. This call to action can be as simple as asking them to review the rest of your business plan or contact you to discuss investment opportunities. As they continue to read the plan, they will have this ask in mind and will be able to form an opinion about how they want to respond based on what you have presented in the rest of your business plan.

Use visuals if it's appropriate:

Consider using a visual element like a graph, chart, or image to make your executive summary more visually engaging and easier to understand. It can also help to make it more memorable. Any easy place to include a visual is in your financial projection snippet in your executive summary. For example, you might include a chart showing the revenue projections of your business for the next two or three years. A chart such as this is much more memorable than writing these projections out in a sentence.

Get a second opinion:

Once you've finished writing your executive summary, it is a good idea to have someone else read it to see if they understand the main points and if it would be interesting for them to read further. Getting feedback from someone unfamiliar with your business can also help you spot any areas that need improvement or areas that need to be clarified.

In general, keep the executive summary short, ideally no more than one or two pages. The goal is to be brief yet include all of the most important information to give your audience a clear understanding of your business and why it is an excellent investment opportunity.

If you have yet to realize it, the executive summary is a crucial component of any business plan and should be written clearly and concisely. It should provide a high-level overview of the most important information about your business and be tailored to the specific audience for which you are writing.

Remember to be brief, but ensure that you provide your audience with the most important information that gives them a clear understanding of your business and why they should invest.

3

HOW TO NAIL YOUR COMPANY DESCRIPTION

The company description portion of your business plan provides a detailed overview of the company and its history, ownership structure, and any relevant background information. Also included in this section is the mission statement, which communicates the company's goals and objectives. As with most sections of your business plan, the company description should be short and snappy yet comprehensive enough to give potential investors and lenders a complete understanding of the company.

HERE ARE THE KEY ELEMENTS YOU MUST INCLUDE WHEN WRITING THE COMPANY DESCRIPTION SECTION OF YOUR BUSINESS PLAN.

Company Name:

Your company's name should be prominently displayed at the top of the section. Make sure it is easy to read and memorable. If you have already pulled together a logo and branding, you should include that in this section. If you have not put this together, then consider investing in this area of your business.

While it may seem daunting or costly, creating a logo for your business is quite simple and can be inexpensive. On platforms like Fiverr and 99designs, you can pay a small amount, anywhere from $50 to $250, and you receive a quality company logo that will give readers of a business plan an excellent impression of you and your business.

I've included a list of my favorite resources at the link here for those who are interested: https://linktr.ee/kaycarroll

Description of the Business:

Your business description should be a brief overview of what your company does and its products or services. It should be clear and concise and explain in simple terms what your company does. Some of the elements to include in this description are:

History of the Company:

This section should include information on when and how the company was founded and any significant milestones or events that have occurred since then. For example, if the company has undergone any significant expansions, rebranding, or changes in ownership, these should be noted.

If the company is brand new, then clearly state that and describe the brief history that the company does have, including the impetus behind starting the business.

Ownership Structure:

This section should include information on the company's ownership structure, such as whether it is a sole proprietorship, partnership, corporation, or limited liability company. If you have partners in the business, then it should also include information on the number of owners, the percentage of ownership they hold, and any relevant background information on the owners.

Be sure also to include information on the company's legal status, such as whether it is registered as a corporation, partnership, or limited liability company. And include any information on any relevant licenses or permits the company holds.

Remember that if you are seeking an equity investment and your business is currently set up as a sole proprietorship, you will likely need to restructure the company to an entity that can take on such investments.

Mission Statement:

A company's mission statement is a short statement that communicates the company's goals and objectives. It should be clear, concise, and easy to understand. A good mission statement conveys the company's purpose and values in a single sentence.

Your mission statement should also be inspiring in that it motivates both employees and investors. Above all, your mission statement should guide your company and truly align with how your company operates. Easy, right?

Organizational Structure:

This section should include information on the company's structure and its different departments or divisions. It should also include information on the company's management and key personnel, including their qualifications and relevant experience.

Again, if your company is new, your organizational structure section will likely be a future state of how you expect the company to be organized. Be sure to include the roles you believe you will need and the time frame in which you will need them.

Being vague here is ok. For example, you might show that you need to hire a Head of Engineering next year, but it's not necessary to note the exact month or quarter for the hire since the timing likely depends on many other things leading up to the making of that hire.

Location:

This section should include information on where the company is located and any relevant information on the location. For example, if the company is located in a specific region or industry cluster, this should be noted.

The location is important for physical businesses that serve customers from a storefront. On the other hand, for a software development company that operates "in the cloud," the location is less important. If you intend to run your company remotely, you will want to let investors know that you can hire the best talent from anywhere in the world and show that you have the experience to manage the team remotely.

Industry:

This section should include a brief overview of the company's industry and its target market. It should also mention the market size and growth of the industry and any trends that are relevant to the company.

As discussed previously, the market size is key because investors and lenders need to know that the opportunity is big enough for you (and them) to make a return on their capital. This also applies to how quickly a market is growing; investors want to see that you are entering a space with ample opportunity to grow and succeed. We will dedicate an entire section of your business plan to industry analysis, so this should provide a brief overview.

When writing the company description, be mindful that the specific elements and content of this section will depend on the type of business you're starting and the needs of your target audience. It is likely that you will have different versions of your business plan with specific versions of your company description that are tailored to certain audiences.

As promised, in each section of this book, we will also go over what you should avoid when writing each portion of your business plan.

AS SUCH, IT IS IMPORTANT TO VOID THE FOLLOWING WHEN WRITING THE COMPANY DESCRIPTION SECTION OF YOUR PLAN:

Being too general:

Avoid using overly general language and ensure the information included is accurate and up-to-date. The company description should be specific and provide a clear and detailed picture of the company.

It should be noted that this is true for nearly every section of your business plan. Therefore, it is imperative that you tailor your offering to each audience.

Neglecting the history of the company:

The company's history, including when and how it was founded and any significant milestones, is important information to include in the company description. Neglecting to include this information can make the company appear less credible.

Further, without a story behind the company, investors are less likely to remember your company.

Ignoring the ownership structure:

Be sure to include information on the company's ownership structure and the owners' backgrounds in the company description. Not incorporating this information can make it difficult for potential investors and lenders to understand the company's management structure.

In general, if your business or if something about your business is confusing, then investors will pass on the opportunity rather than ask clarifying questions. Don't make the decision to pass an easy one for them by failing to include important details.

Failing to include a clear mission statement:

As detailed above, a mission statement is a short statement that communicates the company's goals and objectives. It should be clear, concise, and easy to understand. Failing to include a mission statement can make it difficult for potential investors and lenders to understand the company's purpose and values.

And again, these investors will pass rather than ask any questions.

Not providing enough details on the organizational structure:

The company's organizational structure, including the management and key personnel, is a vital aspect of the company description. Not providing enough details can make it difficult for potential investors and lenders to understand the company's management structure and, therefore, difficult for them to understand how you will be successful.

Neglecting to mention location:

The location of the company and any relevant information about it should be included in the company description. This is especially true for businesses operating physical locations to serve customers. In this scenario, the location will impact every aspect of your business, from operating costs to customer access.

Second, to the executive summary, the company description is the most read portion of any business plan. Think of each successive section of your business plan as an opportunity to hook your reader - they will only continue if they are interested enough in what you are proposing at each step of the way.

SO TO ENSURE THAT YOU STAND OUT FROM THE CROWD, FOLLOW THESE POINTERS WHEN IT COMES TO YOUR COMPANY DESCRIPTION.

Showcase your unique selling proposition (USP):

Highlight what makes your company unique and different from competitors in the market. This will help to make your company stand out and demonstrate why it is a good investment opportunity. In essence, what makes your idea and business proposition different from the hundreds of proposals that your audience has seen?

You need to know your unique selling proposition, and you need to know how to explain your unique selling proposition, which brings us to the next point.

Use storytelling techniques:

Instead of just listing facts and figures, try to use storytelling techniques to capture the reader's attention and imagination. This can make your company description more engaging and memorable.

People don't remember ideas; they remember stories. So if you can truly tell the story of your business and your path forward, then you will capture the attention of your reader, and your pitch is more likely to be successful.

Include testimonials or case studies:

Including testimonials or case studies from satisfied customers can demonstrate the effectiveness of your products or services and build credibility for your company. If you have an established business, then sharing testimonials and stories directly from your customers is the number one way to back up the authenticity of your business.

If you are starting from scratch, any surveys or interviews you have done with potential customers can also be included in this section of your business plan. At the end of the day, investors want to know that your product or service is in demand or will be in demand, and the best way to prove this is by having them hear directly from happy customers.

Highlight your team:

Include information about your management team and key personnel, including their qualifications and relevant experience. Highlighting a solid and experienced team can help to demonstrate the company's potential for success. In the early days of any business, your biggest asset, and potentially your most significant liability, is the team you have assembled to execute the business plan.

Spending some time explaining why you and your team are the perfect group of individuals to transform the vision into a successful business will help ease the worries of those seeking to invest in your business.

Use visuals:

Consider including visual elements such as charts, graphs, or images to make your company description more visually engaging and easier to understand. It can also help to make it more memorable. They say that a picture is worth one thousand words, and this case is no exception.

Share your company's vision and goals:

We discussed this earlier, but it is worth another mention. Be sure to include a section on where the company sees itself in the future and what goals it is working towards; this can help to demonstrate the company's long-term potential and commitment to growth. Further, it will excite the reader and help get them on board with your vision.

Highlight any awards, certifications, or accreditation that the company has earned:

Adding any awards and certifications demonstrates the company's credibility and reputation within the industry. This may also come in the form of awards, certifications, or accreditations earned by the founding team. Remember, a big part of selling any business plan is selling the team behind the business plan as experts, so be sure to include all credentials that you and your team might have.

Mention any partnerships, collaborations, or strategic alliances that the company has established:

Credibility comes in many forms, and having other companies interested in partnering with you is a huge green flag for anyone evaluating your company. This is especially true if the interested partners are successful businesses themselves. If those close to the industry see your company's potential, it is another check in the positive column from the viewpoint of investors.

Share any relevant industry or market analysis:

Later in your business plan, you will elaborate on the industry and market analysis that you have conducted. However, including trends and projections up front in your company description will help to demonstrate the company's understanding of the industry, potential for success, and your knowledge of the space in which you intend to operate.

As we continue through this guide to build your business plan, you will notice some major themes starting to appear. These themes play specific roles in each section of the business plan, so be sure to pay close attention to how best to apply your learnings.

4

SHOWCASING YOUR EXPERTISE WITH AN INDUSTRY ANALYSIS

The industry analysis section of the business plan provides an overview of the industry in which the company operates, including market size, growth rate, trends, and major competitors. It should also include a SWOT analysis highlighting your company's strengths, weaknesses, opportunities, and threats.

Your entire business plan is an opportunity to showcase your expertise, but this section, in particular, should be well-researched and convince your reader that you have a thorough understanding of the industry, which is crucial for creating a realistic and effective business plan as well as for executing on that plan.

Your thoroughly researched industry analysis will also come into play in the next section of your business plan when we assemble your market analysis. Before diving into any particular area of your business plan, it is essential to read through this entire book. In this way, you will know where there is overlap between the sections, and you will save yourself a decent amount of time in the research stage.

WHEN IT COMES TO WRITING THE INDUSTRY ANALYSIS, HERE ARE THE KEY ELEMENTS THAT YOU MUST INCLUDE:

Industry Overview:

As mentioned, this should be a brief overview of the industry, including its size, growth rate, and relevant trends or statistics. It should also include information on the significant segments of the industry and the target market for the company's products or services.

This overview gives the reader a basic understanding of your industry and helps to set the stage for how you intend to enter the market. Without this, many investors unfamiliar with your particular industry may be lost or not understand why your particular approach is relevant.

Market Size and Growth Rate:

This section should include information on the size of the market and its projected growth rate. You can obtain this information from various sources, such as industry reports, government data, and market research firms.

You should have included a slimmed-down version of this in the company overview section of your business plan. This is your opportunity to go into more detail and provide specific data about the overall market and the specific subsection of the market in which you intend to operate. Again, if you are planning to run a brick-and-mortar business, the market size and growth rate should be specific to your industry within your specific market.

Industry Trends:

This section should include information on any relevant trends in the industry, such as changes in consumer behavior, new technologies, or regulation shifts. It's important to note that industry trends can significantly impact the company's operations and should be closely monitored.

When detailing these trends for investors, highlight how your business will tap into these trends and how you either have already or intend to gain a competitive advantage using your knowledge of the trends.

Major Players:

This section should include information on the major players in the industry, including their market share, strengths and weaknesses, and any relevant background information. You can obtain this information from industry reports, annual reports, and other publicly available information.

It is both accepted and expected that your industry will have competitors. Your job is to identify those key players, study them, and craft a plan to out-execute them.

SWOT Analysis:

This should include a detailed analysis of the company's strengths, weaknesses, opportunities, and threats. A SWOT analysis can help identify the company's competitive advantage and potential risks or challenges.

SWOT analysis comes up many times when writing a business plan. As such, I've included a detailed overview of how to approach this type of analysis and a template below.

As it relates to the industry analysis section of your business plan, you will want to run a SWOT analysis for your own company and the major players in your industry. This analysis will help you to identify your best path forward.

First, here are step-by-step instructions for running a SWOT analysis. Next, you will use these instructions to prepare the various SWOT analyses throughout your business plan.

Step 1: Define the Objective

The first step in conducting a SWOT analysis is to define the objective clearly. What are you trying to achieve with this analysis? Are you analyzing a business, a product, a project, or something else? The purpose will be defined by the section of the business plan that you are creating.

Step 2: Identify Strengths

Next, you will identify the strengths of the business, product, or project. What advantages does it have over its competitors? What are the unique selling points? What are the areas in which it excels? List down all the strengths of the subject.

Step 3: Identify Weaknesses

The third step is to identify the weaknesses of the business, product, or project. For example, what are the areas in which it falls short compared to its competitors? What are the potential areas for improvement? What are the drawbacks?

Step 4: Identify Opportunities

The fourth step is to identify the opportunities available to the business, product, or project. For example, what are the emerging trends that the subject can capitalize on? Are there any market gaps? Is there growth potential?

Step 5: Identify Threats

The fifth step is to identify the threats that the business, product, or project faces. For example, what are the potential external factors that could impact the subject negatively? Are there any emerging trends that could pose a threat? Are there any regulatory changes that could have a negative impact?

Step 6: Analyze and Prioritize

The final step is to analyze and prioritize the information you have gathered. Review the list of strengths, weaknesses, opportunities, and threats, and identify the key areas that require attention. Prioritize the most important items and develop a plan of action based on the analysis.

After your analysis, or while conducting your analysis, you will add the details to the template provided below.

The SWOT analysis is not a fancy process, and displaying this information is equally simple.

For ease of use, a digital template is available at the link here: https://linktr.ee/kaycarroll

SWOT ANALYSIS TEMPLATE

Objective: [State the objective of the analysis]

Strengths:

- [List down the strengths of the subject]
- [List down another strength of the subject]
- [Continue listing down all the strengths of the subject]

Weaknesses:

- [List down the weaknesses of the subject]
- [List down another weakness of the subject]
- [Continue listing down all the weaknesses of the subject]

Opportunities:

- [List down the opportunities available to the subject]

- [List down another opportunity available to the subject]
- [Continue listing down all the opportunities available to the subject]

Threats:

- [List down the threats faced by the subject]
- [List down another threat faced by the subject]
- [Continue listing down all the threats faced by the subject]
- Analysis and Prioritization:
- [Review the list of strengths, weaknesses, opportunities, and threats]
- [Identify the key areas that require attention]
- [Prioritize the most important items]
- [Develop a plan of action based on the analysis]

PORTER'S FIVE FORCES ANALYSIS:

Porter's Five Forces Analysis is a framework for industry analysis and business strategy development. It is a tool used to analyze the level of competitive dynamics within an industry and business strategy development.

Before running this analysis, you will have identified the key players in the industry, including suppliers, buyers, competitors, and potential new entrants. Then, to perform Porter's Five Forces Analysis, follow these steps:

1. Analyze the bargaining power of suppliers. This includes factors such as the number and size of suppliers, the uniqueness of their product or service, and their ability to raise prices.
2. Analyze the bargaining power of buyers. This includes factors such as the number and size of buyers, their ability to switch to another product or service, and their ability to negotiate prices.
3. Analyze the threat of new entrants. This includes factors such as the barriers to entry, the cost of entry, and the level of competition in the industry.
4. Analyze the threat of substitute products or services. This includes factors such as the availability and price of substitute products or services.
5. Analyze the intensity of competitive rivalry. This includes factors such as the number of competitors, their market shares, and their ability to innovate and differentiate their products or services.

After analyzing each of these forces, you can use the information gathered to develop a comprehensive understanding of the industry and its level of competitiveness. This can help inform business strategy and decision-making and demonstrate to investors that you understand the industry very deeply.

Barriers to entry:

In your Porter's Five Forces analysis, you will look at this aspect of the market. Still, it's essential to highlight any barriers to entry in the industry, such as economies of scale, capital requirements, and government regulations. Understanding these barriers can help to identify the potential challenges a new entrant may face.

As you write the industry analysis, you should use various sources to gather information, such as industry reports, government data, and market research firms. In your appendix, which we'll cover in a later chapter, you will want to include a list of resources you reference throughout your business plan. Be mindful also that the industry and market can change rapidly, so it's essential to review and update the industry analysis regularly.

NOW THAT WE KNOW WHAT IS REQUIRED IN THIS SECTION, HERE ARE THE BIGGEST MISTAKES THAT PEOPLE MAKE WHEN PUTTING TOGETHER THE INDUSTRY ANALYSIS SECTION OF A BUSINESS PLAN:

Not conducting enough research:

One of the biggest mistakes people make when writing the industry analysis section of a business plan is not conducting enough research. Again, this is a theme that you will hear throughout this book - the more research you do regarding any particular aspect of your business plan, the better off you will be. A thorough understanding of the industry is crucial to create a realistic and effective business plan, so it's important to gather information from various sources and ensure that those sources are reliable.

Not including enough information on competitors:

The industry analysis should include information on the major players in the industry and their market share, strengths, and weaknesses. Failing to have enough information on competitors can make it difficult for potential investors and lenders to understand the competitive landscape. The absence of this analysis will also convey to investors that you have not researched your industry thoroughly.

Not providing current information:

The industry and market can change rapidly, so it is important to ensure that the information included in the industry analysis is up-to-date. In addition, outdated information can lead to faulty analysis and make your business plan less credible.

Further, suppose you are presenting your plan to individuals who are up-to-date on what is happening in your specific market. In that case, you will have lost credibility with those individuals that you may never regain.

Not including a SWOT analysis:

A SWOT analysis can help identify the company's competitive advantage and potential risks or challenges. While it is important for your business plan presentation, the SWOT analysis is arguably more critical for the success of your business.

Failing to include a SWOT analysis will not only make it difficult for potential investors and lenders to understand the company's position in the industry, but it will make it impossible for you to plan effectively for the growth of your business.

Not including Porter's Five Forces Analysis:

As discussed earlier in this chapter, this framework can help to analyze the competitive dynamics of an industry by identifying the five forces within the market: the threat of new entrants, the bargaining power of suppliers, the bargaining power of buyers, the threat of substitutes, and the intensity of competitive rivalry. Not including this relevant analysis is another signal to investors that you have not researched your topic thoroughly enough.

Failing to mention the barriers to entry:

The industry analysis should include information on any barriers to entry into the industry, such as economies of scale, capital requirements, and government regulations. These barriers will be unique to your business and how you intend to operate your business.

Understanding these barriers can help identify the potential challenges a new entrant may face, including you, at the beginning of your venture and how you can "build a moat" around what you intend to build.

Not providing a clear and concise overview:

While you need to be detailed in your analysis, each investor or lender will expect a high-level overview of your industry analysis. This overview should be clear and concise yet comprehensive enough to give potential investors and lenders a complete understanding of the industry. Being too general or including irrelevant information can make the analysis less effective.

AND HERE'S HOW YOU CAN KNOCK YOUR INDUSTRY ANALYSIS OUT OF THE PARK AND PROVE TO YOUR READERS THAT YOU'RE AN EXPERT IN YOUR FIELD:

Identify key industry drivers:

As the expert in your business, identifying and explaining the key factors that drive the industry, such as economic, technological, regulatory, or demographic changes, can help to demonstrate a deep understanding of the industry and make the analysis more robust. Later in your business plan, you will tie those drivers to your approach to your business in a way that will allow you to exploit the drivers and ultimately allow your business to succeed.

Use industry statistics and data to support your analysis:

Nothing is more convincing than incorporating hard data and statistics in the industry analysis and your business plan in general. This will help bolster the analysis's credibility and make it more credible to potential investors and lenders. Additionally, as a business owner, you want to invest your time into something that has the potential to succeed, so this kind of hard evidence should be both necessary and encouraging for you as well.

Provide an analysis of the industry's prospects:

Any good investor and business owner should have a handle on the future of the industry in which they are operating. Only in this way can someone plan for and anticipate impending changes in the market.

Things like expected growth rates, market trends, and future opportunities are all very important for you to understand and ensure that potential investors understand. This helps demonstrate the long-term potential of the industry and the company.

Highlight niche or emerging market segments:

If you can identify and discuss niche or emerging market segments within the industry, then you will surely demonstrate a mastery of your industry that will impress investors. Beyond investors, this mastery will serve you well as you navigate the beginnings of your business and look to scale. The concept of "niching down" is one that many companies use to gain market share and is a very effective way to grow a business.

Discuss any regulatory changes or challenges:

In many industries, regulatory challenges are a key factor in success. As such, the industry analysis should discuss any regulatory changes or challenges that may impact the industry, such as new laws or governmental policies.

These challenges are potential risks to the success of your business. Being upfront about these challenges and putting action plans in place will set you up for success and show investors that you are well-versed in your particular industry.

Use visual elements:

Most people retain information better when it is visually shown to them. Consider including visual elements such as charts, graphs, or images to make the industry analysis more visually engaging and easier to understand. For most people, a chart depicting the industry's potential growth is much more memorable than words on a piece of paper.

Provide a summary and conclusion:

Wrap up this section by summarizing the key points of the analysis in a conclusion section, and provide a clear and concise overview of the industry's current state and prospects. Be sure to hit on the key points that make your business proposal unique within the industry's framework as you conclude this section.

Including these elements and focusing on ways to make your business plan shine in the industry analysis section of the business plan can help to make it stand out and demonstrate a deep understanding of the industry. It can also help to identify potential opportunities and risks and show the long-term potential of the business. These are just some of the elements by which your business plan will be evaluated.

5

PUTTING TOGETHER A SOLID MARKET ANALYSIS

Like the industry analysis, the market analysis is a deep dive into the specific part of the industry where you intend to start and operate your business. This section provides a detailed overview of the target market for your company's products or services, including market size, growth rate, trends, and target customer demographics.

The market analysis should also include a market segmentation analysis that breaks down the market into different segments while also segmenting the target market into smaller groups with similar characteristics. Like all sections of your business plan, this section should be well-researched and demonstrate your thorough understanding of the market, which is crucial for creating a realistic and effective business plan.

WHEN WRITING THE MARKET ANALYSIS, INCLUDING THE FOLLOWING KEY ELEMENTS IS IMPORTANT.

Market Overview:

This section should include a brief overview of the market, including information on the major segments of the market and the target market for the company's products or services. You will dive into more details in each subsequent section of the market analysis. This overview should provide a high-level description, both qualitative and quantitative, of the market and why it is an attractive market in which to start your business.

Market Size and Growth Rate:

Investors are interested in how large the returns on their investment in your business will be. As such, the market size and growth rate are two key elements by which they will judge the potential of your business and, therefore, their investment.

This portion of your market analysis should include information on the size of the market and its projected growth rate. This information can be obtained from various sources, such as industry reports, government data, and market research firms.

As with all research that you are doing concerning your business plan, this should be well-researched and have multiple sources for your information to ensure that your calculations are accurate.

Market Trends:

Understanding your market means understanding the trends within the market. The market trend section of your market analysis should include information about relevant trends in the market, such as changes in consumer behavior, new technologies, or shifts in regulations.

It is important to note that market trends will undoubtedly significantly impact the company's operations and should be closely monitored. Proactively making changes according to these trends will ensure that you are a leader in your space.

Target Customer Demographics:

If you do not know who your customers are, then you should not be in the business in which you are operating.

In your business plan's target customer demographics section, you should include information such as customer age, gender, income, education, location, and any other relevant information. This information can be obtained from various sources, such as market research studies, surveys, and focus groups.

It is your job to ensure that your product or service offering is attractive to the set of customers that you are targeting. If it is not appealing to these customers, you have two options: change your offering or find a target customer that wants your solution.

Market Segmentation:

This section should include a detailed market segmentation analysis, which breaks down the market into different segments and segments the target market into smaller groups with similar characteristics.

Going through this analysis should help you identify the market's most profitable segments and tailor the company's products or services to meet their specific needs. This should also aid you in understanding your target customer demographics.

Competitive Analysis:

Similar to the process you went through in the industry analysis, a competitive analysis of your specific market should include information on the major competitors and their market share, strengths, and weaknesses. It is a good idea to run a SWOT analysis on each of your competitors to understand what you are up against.

You should be able to find this information in industry reports, annual reports, and other publicly available information. A quick Google search will reveal much of the information you need.

Market SWOT Analysis:

If you have yet to realize it, you will be running multiple SWOT analyses while writing your business plan. We previously provided a detailed explanation of how to run this type of analysis, along with a template for a SWOT analysis.

This particular SWOT analysis should include a detailed analysis of the company's strengths, weaknesses, opportunities, and threats concerning the market. This will help you identify your company's competitive advantage and potential risks or challenges.

Sales and Marketing Strategies:

Completing the previous subsections of your market analysis should have prepared you for your plan's sales and marketing strategy section. This section will include a discussion of the company's sales and marketing strategies, including how it plans to reach and market to its target customers, which you previously identified. You will elaborate on your sales and marketing plans later in your business plan, so offering a high-level summary here will preview what is to come later in your business plan.

AS YOU PUT THE MARKET ANALYSIS SECTION OF YOUR BUSINESS PLAN TOGETHER, HERE ARE THE BIGGEST PITFALLS TO AVOID WHILE YOU WORK THROUGH THIS PROCESS:

Not conducting enough research:

We will hit on this a few more times throughout this book. One of the biggest mistakes people make when creating a market analysis is not conducting enough research. I will not belabor this point any longer, for now.

Not including enough information on competitors:

There are competitors at the industry level and your specific market level. The market analysis should include information on the major competitors in the market to ensure that you, and the investors from whom you are seeking funding, know what to expect and how to approach the market.

Not providing current information:

Business moves quickly. The market can change rapidly, so it's important to ensure that the information in the market analysis is up-to-date. Outdated information can lead to faulty analysis and make your business plan less credible.

Not including clear target customer demographics:

Not knowing your customer and not knowing how to approach your customer is a huge red flag for anyone evaluating a business plan. The market analysis must include previously discussed information about the target customer demographics, such as age, gender, income, education, location, and any other relevant information.

Not providing realistic projections and growth rates:

While investors want to be part of something with big potential, these same investors can also discern when projections are inaccurate. It is important to be honest and realistic when writing the market analysis and not to exaggerate the size or growth potential of the market too much. Exaggeration on this front will only lead to difficult conversations later when your business comes nowhere near the promised targets.

Not including sales and marketing strategies:

Your sales and marketing strategies are the culmination of all the research you have done on the industry, the market, and your target customers. You must demonstrate to those reading your business plan that you know how to attract and retain the customers you are targeting.

NOW THAT YOU KNOW WHAT TO AVOID WHEN RUNNING A PROPER ANALYSIS OF THE MARKET, WE WILL COVER WAYS TO ENSURE THAT YOU PREPARE THE BEST ANALYSIS POSSIBLE.

Include a detailed customer persona:

As we discussed, knowing your customer is one of the most important aspects of any business plan. As such, creating a detailed customer persona, a fictional representation of your company's ideal customer, will help you stand out.

Be sure to include information such as demographics, pain points, goals, and behaviors. This can help you better understand and communicate your target market and ensure that your market analysis is more relatable and memorable.

Use surveys and customer feedback:

If you are already operating your business, then including feedback and data from surveys or customer interviews in the market analysis will help hammer home your demonstration of your understanding of your customers.

These types of surveys and feedback loops are also hugely valuable tools for you as a business owner. They can provide insights into customer needs and preferences, allowing you to tailor your offering appropriately.

Identify untapped market segments:

Big businesses can be built by tapping into new segments of a particular market.

This is simply defined as markets within your industry that have not been addressed and to which you can apply your tried and true business model. With investors, this can help to demonstrate the company's ability to identify new opportunities and innovate in the market. For your business, this will be invaluable when it comes to generating additional revenue and growing your company.

Use visual elements:

Another consistent theme throughout your business plan should be the use of visual elements such as charts, graphs, or images to make the market analysis more visually engaging and easier to understand. Again, leaving readers with a visual will also help ensure your presentation is more memorable.

Provide a market segmentation analysis:

By this, I mean that you should break down the market into different segments and segment your target market into smaller groups with similar characteristics.

Going through this exercise in conjunction with truly understanding your target customers will help you identify the market's most profitable segments and tailor the company's products or services to meet their specific needs.

Demonstrating your knowledge and ability to run this kind of segmentation analysis will help your pitch when presenting your business plan to investors and lenders.

Include a discussion of the industry's trends and prospects:

When putting together a business plan, you want to look at the current state of the business and the future state of the business and the industry. Discussing the industry's trends and prospects concerning the market, such as expected growth rates, market trends, and future opportunities, will help to demonstrate the long-term potential of the industry and the company.

Provide a summary and conclusion:

This is a seemingly minor point, but summarizing the key points of the analysis in a conclusion section and providing a clear and concise overview of this section of your business plan will help tie things together simply for readers.

Include a discussion of the marketing strategy and budget:

We will cover the financial section of your business plan in a later chapter. Still, it is wise to include in your market analysis a detailed explanation of how the company plans to reach and market to its target customers, including a breakdown of the budget and the projected return on investment. Keeping the financial impacts of the strategy close to where you are explaining the strategies will keep any confusion to a minimum.

As with all of the research that goes into your business plan, when writing the market analysis, it's essential to use various sources to gather information, such as industry reports, government data, and market research firms.

While tempting to inflate market potential in your business plan, it is also important to be honest and realistic when writing the market analysis and not to exaggerate the size or growth potential of the market. Provide realistic projections and growth rates based on your research. This does not mean you cannot dream but dream within reason.

It is also essential to keep in mind that the market can change rapidly, so it is essential to regularly review and update the market analysis, even when you are not looking for additional investments. Written well, your business plan will help you to build as you scale, and as such, your business plan should be a living document within your organization.

6

DEMONSTRATING YOUR KNOWLEDGE OF THE SPACE WITH A COMPETITIVE ANALYSIS

This chapter will delve into the crucial process of conducting a competitive analysis for your business. A competitive analysis will help you understand the strengths and weaknesses of your competitors, provide valuable insights into the marketplace, and allow you to craft your approach accordingly.

By conducting a thorough analysis of your competitors, you can determine your unique value proposition and develop strategies to gain the upper hand over your competitors. Whether you're just starting a business or looking to expand your existing one, this chapter will provide a step-by-step guide on running a competitive analysis and making informed decisions for your business.

NOW, WE'LL COVER THE KEY ELEMENTS THAT SHOULD BE INCLUDED WHEN WRITING THE COMPETITIVE ANALYSIS SECTION OF A BUSINESS PLAN.

Identify direct and indirect competitors:

Be sure to identify both direct and indirect competitors, including their market share, strengths, and weaknesses of those competitors. Direct competitors are companies that offer similar products or services to what you offer.

Indirect competitors offer substitute products or services.

For example, the direct competitor of a donut shop could be another local donut shop offering similar types of donuts and refreshments. On the other hand, an indirect competitor of a donut shop could be a bagel shop that also serves customers during breakfast hours with accompanying refreshments. These businesses serve the same market and need but offer different products.

Analyze their marketing strategies:

Similar to how you crafted and analyzed your marketing strategies, it is wise also to analyze the competitors' marketing strategies, including their target market, pricing strategy, and promotional tactics. For example, you may take away from this process that your competitors are lost, or you may learn something applicable to your approach, thereby enhancing your business.

Assess their strengths and weaknesses:

In the same way, you assessed your strengths and weaknesses; you must run the same analysis on your competitors, including their financial stability, reputation, and brand recognition. Going through this process will open your eyes to any advantages you have over your competitors and any potential challenges you need to address with your own business.

To ensure that you cover all of the details in this, we suggest conducting a SWOT analysis of each of the major competitors to your business. In this way, you will truly understand where your business stands in the marketplace and be able to adjust your business to be the market leader.

Evaluate their competitive position:

Dig further into your competitor and how their position in the market relates to the position of your business. With each evaluation of your competitors, you will learn more and more about the advantages that you have as well as any weaknesses that you have relative to those with whom you are competing. In this case, turning a blind eye to the competition will very rarely lead to a positive outcome for your business.

Look at the Industry trends:

As almost a subsection of your competitive analysis, you will want to evaluate how industry trends will impact the competitive landscape for your business.

In the example of the donut shop that we used earlier, if there is a trend in the market towards healthier breakfast options, then the donut shop might begin to offer more nutritious versions of their favorite donuts to keep customers walking through the door despite that latest health craze.

Provide a summary and conclusion:

As is a theme with nearly all sections of your business plan, you must summarize the key points of the competitive analysis in a conclusion section and provide a clear and concise overview of the competition's current state and prospects. Providing a proper action plan on how the company plans to address its competition and maintain its competitive advantage is also a wise thing to do when wrapping up this section of your plan.

NOW, ON TO THE BIGGEST MISTAKES TO AVOID WHEN COMPILING YOUR COMPETITIVE ANALYSIS.

Not conducting enough research:

If we've said it once, then we've said it one hundred times - your business plan is only as good as the research and thought you put into it. One of the most common mistakes people make when creating a competitive analysis is not conducting enough research. A thorough understanding of the competitive landscape is crucial to create a realistic and effective business plan, so it is important to gather information from various sources.

Not identifying all the competitors:

Ignoring competition, whether it be in your business plan or as you are operating your business, does not make that competition disappear. In this entire section dedicated to competitive analysis for your business, it is very important to include information on all the major competitors in the market, not just the direct ones. Failing to identify all the competitors can lead to an incomplete understanding of the competitive landscape and make your business plan both less credible and, for lack of a better word, useless.

Not providing current information:

Your research on the competitive landscape can quickly become outdated, so it is important to ensure that the information included in the competitive analysis is up-to-date. Obsolete information can lead to faulty analysis, which will lead to an approach that will not work for the current state of the market.

Not providing realistic market share information:

As previously mentioned, giving your investors a glimpse into the dream scenario for your business is great. Still, it is essential to be honest and realistic when writing each section of your business plan. There is no need to exaggerate the company's market share or downplay the competition's market share too much. Be sure to provide realistic market share information based on your research.

Not including a discussion of the industry's trends and prospects:

Ignoring industry trends as they relate to your competition and your prospects is akin to ignoring competition altogether. As discussed above, including a discussion of the industry's trends and future prospects, such as expected growth rates, market trends, and future opportunities, will help you demonstrate the long-term potential of the industry and the company.

Not including a discussion of the company's competitive strategy:

It seems like we should not have to point this one out, but the competitive analysis should also include a discussion of your company's competitive strategy, including how the company plans to maintain its competitive advantage and address its competition.

AND HERE'S HOW YOU CAN PUT YOURSELF IN A GOOD POSITION TO SUCCEED WHEN CONDUCTING YOUR COMPETITIVE ANALYSIS.

Thorough research:

Research is the basis on which you are building a large part of your business and this business plan. A competitive analysis based on thorough research, including data from various sources, such as industry reports, company websites, and financial statements, is the only way to provide a complete and accurate understanding of the competitive landscape.

In-depth analysis:

After conducting all required research, you must spend the time to analyze your competitors in-depth. You should know their businesses almost as well as they know their businesses. In this way, you will set yourself apart from the competition and truly set your business up to be agile.

Detailed market segmentation:

A competitive analysis that includes detailed market segmentation breaking down the market into smaller groups with similar characteristics can help identify the market's most profitable segments and tailor the company's products or services to meet their specific needs. Much like it is important to understand your customers, it is also important to understand the customers of your competitors such that you can win these customers in the long run.

Clear and concise language:

This is the first time we have mentioned this, but it applies to every section of your business plan. Writing in clear and concise language, and using visual elements such as charts and graphs, will ensure that you are fully understood by whoever is reading your business plan.

Most investors are not impressed by the use of big words. They are more interested in understanding how a business operates and whether it has ample opportunity ahead of it. Further, a clear and consistent format, with a logical flow of information, can make it easier for the reader to understand and follow.

As always, be honest and realistic when writing the competitive analysis, and do not exaggerate the company's competitive advantage or downplay the competition.

7

BUILDING A SALES AND MARKETING PLAN TO BEAT YOUR COMPETITION

A well-crafted sales and marketing plan will undoubtedly take your business to the next level. This plan is a crucial aspect of the success of any business and, if done well, can lead to revenue as you've never thought possible.

A sales and marketing plan helps define your target audience and establish a clear understanding of your unique value proposition, and provides a roadmap for effectively reaching and engaging with potential customers. Let's repeat that. As a business owner and operator, you must effectively and efficiently engage with potential customers.

A solid plan can drive growth and increase revenue by maximizing your resources and efforts, enabling you to stay ahead of the competition and continuously adapt to the changing market landscape. Regardless of whether you're starting a new business or looking to grow your existing business, investing your time and dollars into a comprehensive sales and marketing plan is a vital step toward realizing your vision and achieving your goals.

At its core, a sales and marketing plan outlines the strategies and tactics that your company will use to reach and market to its target customers.

WHEN WRITING THE SALES AND MARKETING PLAN TO INCLUDE IN YOUR BUSINESS PLAN, IT IS ESSENTIAL TO INCLUDE THE FOLLOWING KEY ELEMENTS AND TO DEMONSTRATE HOW YOUR PLAN WILL POSITIVELY IMPACT REVENUE.

Target market:

You will have already defined your target market in previous exercises, so this overview should be tailored to how your target market will dictate your sales and marketing plans. Again, clearly define the target market, including demographics, psychographics, and buying behavior.

You will then need to provide details on how to approach this target market, and segments of this market, thereby demonstrating that you have crafted an approach that will work. This information that you gather around your market segments will help you understand which segments are the most profitable and ultimately will allow you to tailor the company's products or services to meet their specific needs.

Competitive advantage:

With respect to your sales and marketing plan, your competitive advantage lies in identifying your company's unique selling proposition (USP) and demonstrating how you will communicate that to the target market. This unique selling proposition can help to differentiate your company from its competitors and make it more attractive to potential customers.

If we continue with the Donut Shop example from the previous section, some USPs could be:

- Fresh, made-to-order donuts: emphasizing the quality and freshness of the donuts offered, potentially using terms like "handcrafted" or "baked-on-site."
- Wide variety of flavors: highlighting the extensive selection of flavors, focusing on unique or seasonal options.

- Eco-friendly packaging: positioning the donut shop as environmentally conscious by offering biodegradable or recyclable packaging options.

These unique selling propositions should, of course, be tailored to your target market. For example, if you are highlighting eco-friendly packaging to a market that cares only about the price of a donut, then your marketing plan will likely fail.

As you might be learning, the key to a large portion of the pieces of your business is to truly understand the wants and needs of your customers - whoever that might be.

Product or service offering:

Your sales and marketing strategy should clearly describe your company's products or services, including features, benefits, and pricing. Specifically, you must explain this information, highlighting the value you are bringing to your target market and your customers.

The ability to clearly describe your product offering to investors in your business plan will prove that you have a handle on how to market your products or services to your potential customer base. On the contrary, if you have trouble simplifying your product or service offering in your business plan, then those reading the plan will wonder how you will do this for your potential customers.

Sales strategy:

Sales are about the pipeline you can create, and whether you are in software sales or the donut business, sales are the lifeblood of your company. In short, your company will cease to exist if you are not selling.

Your sales strategy should outline how your company plans to generate leads and convert those leads into customers. This can include information on the sales process, sales channels, and sales team. This also closely connects with the next section of your business plan - your marketing strategy.

Marketing strategy:

At a high level, your marketing strategy should outline how the company plans to reach and communicate with its target market. Depending on the type of business you are engaged in, this will look very different and can include information on marketing channels, campaigns, and budgets.

Within your marketing strategy, you must outline the different approaches you will use when addressing your target market. Depending on the type of business that you operate, your marketing strategy may or may not include a combination of the following:

Advertising and Promotion:

At the highest level, this is how you intend to communicate with your target market via different media channels, including direct mail, TV advertisements, local newspapers, and various other channels. It is your responsibility to truly understand where your customers are so that you can meet them in those places.

For example, with your local Donut Shop, you might advertise in the local newspaper or run a radio ad that is localized to your area to promote your business. You should not, however, run a national TV campaign because advertising to a group of customers who cannot travel to your physical location when you operate your Donut Shop is, for lack of a better word, useless.

Public Relations:

In certain businesses, public relations will be required. Specifically, you need to build and maintain a positive public reputation with the target market. This public relation plan would include information on media relations, events, and crisis management information. It is up to you to determine whether a public relations plan is needed for your particular business.

Digital Marketing:

Digital marketing, or performance marketing, is crucial to the success of any business, so outlining this strategy in your marketing plan is very important. In this section of your plan, be sure to include how the company plans to reach and communicate with the target market through digital channels like Facebook, Instagram, Tik Tok, and YouTube.

This can also include information on the website, search engine optimization (SEO), email marketing, and online advertising. You must focus on platforms where your customers spend time, meaning that it probably wouldn't be wise to spend money on Tik Tok if your target market was born before 1950.

TO DEMONSTRATE THE POWER OF DIGITAL MARKETING, WE'LL CONTINUE WITH OUR DONUT SHOP EXAMPLE.

In this example, your donut shop is serving a local audience, and your marketing strategy will also be localized. Specifically, focusing on social media platforms like Facebook would be wise as they allow you to target your audience based on local and demographics.

Through your target customer research, you know your audience will likely be families, students, and office workers. Use this information to set up targeted social media campaigns that drive customers to your store.

To understand whether your social media campaigns are operating efficiently, consider including a coupon code with your campaigns. In this way, you can measure the sales that came from the coupon you advertised against the money you spent on your social media advertisements.

Measuring and monitoring progress:

You will only be as good as what you measure. As such, setting up key performance indicators (KPIs) to guide each portion of your business, and specifically your sales and marketing plan, is key to your success. This will allow you to measure and monitor the progress of the actions that you are taking. More specifically, your KPIs and metrics should inform you whether a particular strategy is working for your business.

From our Facebook advertisement discussion around our donut shop, the KPI we were focusing on was return on investment (ROI) related to money spent on Facebook advertisement.

For example, if you spent $100 on Facebook advertisements that only brought in $5 of business, then your ROI is low. If you spent $100 on Facebook advertisements that brought in $500 of business, then your ROI is high.

Even if you were to break even on what your advertisements brought in, then you're in a good position because there are residual effects that boost your brand that come by way of this advertisement, and if you see an overall increase in sales when you are running these campaigns, then it is likely that this organic lift came as a result of your advertisements.

Budgeting and forecasting:

In the budgeting and forecasting portion of your marketing plan, you should include forecasting for the projected costs and revenue resulting from your marketing plan.

Provide cost estimates for each channel through which you intend to advertise and the expected return from those costs in the form of revenue for your business.

Be specific about the timing of your marketing efforts, including when you are advertising on each channel and why it makes sense to advertise during that time.

Finally, use the metrics you defined previously to measure the success of each campaign and to determine in which channels you should continuously invest.

This will demonstrate to potential investors the financial feasibility of the plan and provide a clear picture of the company's projected growth.

THE COMMON MISTAKES THAT PEOPLE RUN INTO WHEN PUTTING TOGETHER A SALES AND MARKETING PLAN ARE PRETTY SIMILAR TO THE ERRORS THAT ARE MADE IN ANY PORTION OF THE BUSINESS PLAN, SO WE'LL COVER JUST A FEW HERE.

Not defining the target market:

Without a target market, as it relates to your sales and marketing strategies, it is impossible to create an advertising plan because you have no idea to whom you are speaking and what interests them. You must understand who your customers are, including their demographics, psychographics, and buying behavior, to create an effective plan for reaching and marketing to them.

Not identifying a unique selling proposition:

Without a unique selling proposition, your donut shop will look like every other donut shop in town, and you will not be able to leverage anything differentiating to bring customers through your door versus the donut shop down the street.

As such, you need to clearly understand what sets your company apart from its competitors and craft your sales and marketing strategy around how that differentiator will be communicated to your target customers.

Not providing enough detail on the product or service:

Nothing is worse than a vague advertisement that does not properly communicate what your product is and what it can do for your customers. Any solid sales and marketing plan should include detailed information on the company's products or services, including features, benefits, and pricing.

The only exception here is that sometimes pricing is not required in advertisements, but this will depend on your target customer and the product or service you provide. That said, without enough detail on your product or service in your business plan, it can be difficult for potential investors and lenders to understand your company's value proposition and how it meets the needs of your target market.

Not providing a clear and realistic sales strategy:

As with all portions of your business plan, your sales strategy should be clearly outlined, optimistic, and realistic. Include details on how your company intends to generate leads and convert those leads into customers. Excluding this from your sales and marketing plan will leave investors asking questions about whether or not your company can indeed generate revenue.

Not providing a clear and realistic marketing strategy:

Similar to your sales strategy, your marketing strategy should be very clear and include details on how you plan to reach and communicate with the target market. A lack of a marketing plan will leave investors asking whether you can grow your business sustainably and efficiently.

Additionally, leaving out a strategy that focuses on digital marketing is a surefire way to demonstrate that you are not fit to run a business. In today's environment, a digital marketing approach is essential to the success of your business. Think about it this way, when you are looking for a solution to your sugar craving, the first place you go is Google. If our theoretical donut shop shows up nowhere when someone searches for "sweet treats near me," then you have no chance of acquiring that customer.

Not including budgeting and forecasting:

As painful and tedious as it might be to put together a budget for your marketing plan, you will be thankful that you did. Understanding the costs and potential revenue associated with your business will allow you to make knowledgeable decisions for your company.

For example, a plan to spend hundreds of thousands of dollars on a billboard might get you a lot of exposure, but if said billboards do not lead to increased sales, then you are dead in the water.

Not including a plan to measure and monitor progress:

Measuring your progress against your forecast will allow you to make real-time decisions about whether or not a particular campaign is working for your business. Specifically, measuring the ROI as it relates to your digital campaigns on a daily or weekly basis will let you pivot your spending to more successful campaigns and reduce spending on campaigns that seem to be losing money for your business.

As such, your sales and marketing plan must include a plan for measuring and monitoring progress, including deliberately chosen KPIs and metrics. Without this information, you will have no way of tracking progress and making adjustments as needed.

NOW TO DIFFERENTIATE YOURSELF FROM THE CROWD WHEN IT COMES TO YOUR SALES AND MARKETING PLAN, HERE ARE THE TOP METHODS THROUGH WHICH YOU CAN ACHIEVE THIS.

Conduct thorough market research:

As it relates to your sales and marketing plan, understanding your market completely is absolutely critical. Read industry reports, conduct surveys of your current or potential customers, and talk to as many people as you possibly can.

By having hundreds of conversations with people who could be your customer, you will narrow in on how best to approach that customer. Talking to your customers is the secret sauce to providing a product or service that meets their needs. Most business owners shy away from this part of the process, but you are not most business owners.

Identify unique and creative marketing strategies:

After speaking with as many customers as possible, you will be able to identify unique selling points around your product offering using your customers' words.

You may learn that a loyalty and referral program is the missing piece that your customers are craving. By advertising your new loyalty program, you will set yourself apart from your competitors and improve your sales.

Your creative marketing strategies might include utilizing new technologies, like AI, to craft proper marketing messaging specific to different market segments or implementing a direct mail campaign to a very specific zip code within your market. The more specific you get, the more you will learn from each campaign.

Use visual elements:

Visual elements are usually more attention-grabbing than just using words in a marketing campaign. In a world where people are bombarded with new products and services each and every day, one eye-catching visual might stick with people, capturing their attention and getting them to engage with your business over another. These elements also tend to evoke emotions more than plain text, which can help to build a connection between your customers and your brand.

Finally, visuals allow you to tell a better story about your business and bring a brand message to life in a way that words alone cannot. If your marketing elements are doing this for your customers, they will accomplish the same for your potential investors, which is precisely the outcome you are looking for.

Provide clear and specific goals and action plan:

Having a plan with clear and specific goals brings a lot of key things to your business. Specifically, this type of plan provides focus and aligns the marketing plan to the overall company objectives, ensuring that resources are used effectively.

Additionally, with a clear action plan comes measurable results, and by evaluating those results regularly, you can adjust your plan to keep your company moving in the right direction. Nearly all businesses are resource constrained, and having a clear plan of action when it comes to marketing will allow you to prioritize where to spend time and money in the most impactful way for the business.

Show evidence of past success in your marketing messaging:

One powerful way to show evidence of past success is to use testimonials and case studies from customers who have experienced the benefits of your products.

Hearing from people who have used and benefited from your product is the number one way to drive additional customers to your business because someone other than the company is sharing about the benefits, which brings instant credibility to your company.

For investors, these types of testimonials provide the same credibility and demonstrate your ability to execute your sales and marketing strategy, building trust with potential investors and lenders.

Show adaptability to change:

I cannot overemphasize the importance of adaptability in your business. The strategies that worked for you last year to drive business will likely fail this year. As such, your ability to understand changes in the market, the economy, and other external factors that impact your business is key to your survival.

Demonstrating an ability to adapt your plan to these changes with measurable results will show that your company is well-positioned to navigate the uncertainties of the business and make necessary changes to ensure success.

A well-written and thoroughly researched sales and marketing plan is crucial for the success of your business and is an essential element of any business plan.

This plan outlines all of your strategies, tying them together in one cohesive plan that demonstrates your ability to effectively and efficiently win customers for your business. Every plan must be unique, and it is up to you to find the secret weapons that differentiate your business from your competitors.

8

DESCRIBING THE SERVICE OR PRODUCT THAT YOU ARE OFFERING

To begin, I want to give a template paragraph for incorporating all of the elements required when building this section of your business plan. Before you continue reading, use this template to write about your business. It is okay to leave certain portions blank, as you should be able to fill them out by the end of this chapter.

"We are excited to introduce [Company Name], a provider of [product/service]. Our [product/service] is designed to [provide a solution/address a need]. With [unique feature/benefit], we are confident that our [product/service] will be the [ideal solution/answer] for [target audience/customer need]. Our team of experts has [years of experience/unique qualifications] and is dedicated to delivering [high-quality/exceptional] [product/service]. Whether you're looking for [specific

feature/benefit], we have the [product/service] that will [provide a solution/meet your needs]. We invite you to learn more about [Company Name] and our [product/service] today."

The product and service description section is a crucial component of your business plan. It outlines your company's offerings and how they meet the target market's needs. We will break down each portion of this template description, and by the end of this chapter, you will have a solid description based on the paragraph that was shared above.

WHEN WRITING THE SERVICE OR PRODUCT LINE PORTION OF A BUSINESS PLAN, IT'S IMPORTANT TO INCLUDE THE FOLLOWING KEY ELEMENTS:

Product or service description:

Your business plan should clearly describe your company's products or services, including a detailed explanation of their features and benefits. Present this information in a very simple way to understand, and that highlights the value of the offering to the target market.

For our donut shop, this might be a solid description of products and services:

Indulge in a symphony of flavors with every bite at Kay's Donuts. Our handcrafted donuts are more than just a sweet treat; they're a work of art. Each donut is carefully crafted with the finest ingredients, from rich and creamy fillings to delicate and flaky crusts. Whether you prefer the classic taste of a glazed donut or the bold flavors of our specialty creations, every bite is a burst of delight for your taste buds. Our donuts are made fresh daily, ensuring that you experience the perfect combination of texture and flavor in every bite. Come visit us and treat yourself to a taste of heaven at Kay's Donuts.

A warranty or guarantee might accompany a purchase of certain products and services.

In these cases, be sure to include a product or service warranty or guarantee, including the terms and conditions. These types of guarantees will help build trust with potential customers and, for potential investors, will demonstrate your commitment to customer satisfaction through quality assurance.

Competitive analysis:

For both yourself and potential investors, a comparative analysis of your products against your competitors will help clarify your unique selling proposition and how you differentiate your offerings from your competition.

An analysis of Kay's Donut shop against local competitors might include the following:

- Product offering comparison: comparing the types of donuts provided, including the number of flavors, specialty options, and seasonal offerings.
- Quality of ingredients: comparing the quality of the ingredients that go into the donuts from each shop, like the type of flower, sugar, and fillings.
- Taste and texture: comparing the taste and texture of the donuts from each shop, including the level of sweetness, the consistency of the dough, and the flavor of the fillings.
- Price: Compare the prices of the donuts at each shop, including the cost of individual donuts, boxes, and other products.
- Location and convenience: Compare the locations and convenience of each shop, including accessibility, parking, and hours of operation.
- Customer service: Compare the customer service experience at each shop, including the friendliness of the staff, the speed of service, and the availability of seating.

- Marketing and branding: Compare the marketing and branding efforts of each shop, including the use of social media, advertising, and community events.
- Reputation: Compare the reputation of each shop, including customer reviews and ratings, word of mouth, and industry awards.

While this can be very subjective, when you are meeting with investors, you can also bring in physical products from your business and your competitors. In this way, you can demonstrate the differences you highlighted in your competitive analysis.

Market segmentation:

Using the work you did previously around market segmentation, you should use this section to describe how your company's products or services meet the specific needs of each segment. Doing so will help to position yourself as the best business to address each market segment.

Suppose that one of the market segments for Kay's Donuts was individuals who work in office environments. By highlighting the baker's dozen loyalty program that your donut shop created, you will show how you effectively bring these customers back week after week to purchase donuts for their officemates.

Product or service development:

The product or service you provide may or may not be proprietary, but in either instance, you will need to explain the process through which you develop your product or service in your business plan. If you're manufacturing something, this could include research and development, testing, and quality control. On the other hand, this could simply be a description of how you honed in on the successful service model you're utilizing.

Depending on what you provide, this section of your business plan may be very short or quite extensive. It is up to you to decide what you need to demonstrate your development process.

Pricing strategy:

In some cases, innovative pricing is the competitive edge on which the business relies to gain and retain market share. In this section, you will outline your pricing strategy, including the many factors that went into determining the pricing for your offering.

Oftentimes this includes information on costs, competition, and your target market.

This might also include an explanation of an innovative pricing strategy that you're using, such as bringing subscription pricing to an industry that typically does not use this pricing model.

Distribution and delivery:

A key component of your business is how said business makes its product or service available to potential customers. For businesses where physical goods are sold to customers, this will include a description of physical locations or the supply chain through which products are delivered to customers. For online platforms, this might be as simple as detailing the simplicity of how customers will log in to your application to access your product.

Intellectual property protection:

Not all businesses will develop or rely on intellectual property, but in many cases, companies will at least have a trademarked logo. In this section, list and describe any of your intellectual property, including patents, trademarks, and copyrights. Also, include any legal documents associated with the intellectual property you claim. This will help to demonstrate your commitment to protecting the company from any legal issues that could arise.

Supporting materials:

Throughout your business plan, including this section, it is important to include any supporting materials for your description. For example, if you are describing your products, including photos or videos of product demonstrations will help to tie the different portions of your business plan together in one complete picture.

Scalability:

Providing any product or service requires work and effort on the part of a team or machines. To meet the sales targets you previously described, you will need to demonstrate your ability to scale the creation of your product or service as demand increases.

Along with this scale will come costs, so showing investors that you've planned for those costs and that you understand how those costs impact the margins of the business will go a long way in building trust in your plan.

WE'LL NOW REVIEW THE TOP MISTAKES THAT BUSINESS OWNERS MAKE WHEN DETAILING THEIR SERVICE OR PRODUCT LINES IN THEIR BUSINESS PLANS.

Not clearly defining the product or service:

As a business owner, you undoubtedly have more context about your product or service offering than anyone in the world. As such, you will often make assumptions about what people know or do not know about your business. Clearly defining your product or service for the reader of your business plan, including even the most mundane details, is hugely important.

This includes ensuring that you provide enough detail on the features, benefits, and pricing of the product or service in a way that makes it simple for investors and lenders to understand the value proposition and how it meets the needs of the target market.

Not providing a competitive analysis:

We've discussed this previously, and we'll remind you again later ignoring the presence of competition does not make your business look stronger.

In fact, by not providing a competitive analysis specific to the products or services you provide, you're doing yourself a disservice as you attempt to grow your business and as you are looking for capital from investors and lenders.

In order to become comfortable with an investment, all investors will want to know how your products or services stack up against others in the market and what you are doing to improve your standing.

Not describing the product or service development process:

Omitting this section of your business plan might seem trivial; however, doing so will create some concern over how well you understand your business and, therefore, how well you will be able to adapt to any changes that might come your way.

Use this section to show your mastery of not only what you sell but how you develop what it is that you sell. In cases where you've put in years of research and development, put that on display in your business plan to show that new entrants in the market will have a long way to go before they get to your level of expertise.

Not providing a distribution and delivery plan:

Arguably as important as the product or service that you're selling is how you distribute that product or service. You've already outlined how you intend to capture customers, so this is your opportunity to demonstrate how you will ensure that these customers get what they came for. Disregarding this detail happens often and only leads to questions from anyone looking at your business plan.

Not considering scalability:

Investors and lenders are interested in companies that show the ability for growth. The simple reason is that investors and lenders want to understand how they will benefit financially from their investment. If these same investors don't see a path for you to meet your sales goals via the scalability of your business, then they will be less likely to invest their money in you and your business.

AND HERE ARE WAYS TO HELP DIFFERENTIATE YOUR BUSINESS WHEN EXPLAINING YOUR SERVICE OR PRODUCT LINE.

Identify a unique selling proposition:

Your unique selling proposition (USP) or competitive advantage is what makes your business different from other companies that are serving your target market.

Sometimes this is your pricing model; other times, it is a particular product feature. Regardless, emphasizing your USP in the description of your product or service will help to generate excitement amongst potential investors.

Use unique branding and packaging:

As much as we're taught not to judge a book by its cover, in many instances, the only product differentiator that you have is what your branding or packaging looks like. Creating something unique that will stand out when a customer is searching the web for a solution or standing in the aisle of their favorite retailer will help to differentiate your company's products or services and make them more memorable to potential customers.

Offer a superior level of customer service:

As a customer, waiting on hold when seeking an answer to your question is potentially the most frustrating part of doing business with a company. Companies that offer superior customer service, like the service provided by Zappos with 24/7 phone support and friendly employees, can be a powerful differentiator, particularly in service-based industries, but across all types of businesses.

Suppose your prices are slightly higher than a competitor, but your customer service is highly personal, fast, and friendly. In that case, your customer retention will be unmatched, and your potential as a company will be sky-high.

This kind of service will undoubtedly build a loyal customer base, which is the heart of any successful business. By creating a positive customer experience, providing excellent customer service, and developing long-lasting relationships, your business can create a loyal customer base that will drive repeat business and attract new customers through word-of-mouth.

Create a strong digital presence and leverage technology:

Irrespective of whether you're operating a brick-and-mortar business or a business that operates solely online, creating a strong digital presence will ensure that your business is more visible and accessible to your customers. When searching for a solution to their needs, people either ask a trusted friend or take to the Internet. By investing in search engine optimization, an easy-to-navigate website, and email marketing campaigns, you'll be top of mind for your potential customers.

Hand in hand with your digital presence is the technology you utilize in your business.

You will level up your business without adding much overhead by incorporating automation, artificial intelligence, and the many technology platforms out there.

Creating a green or sustainable business:

While not required, creating green policies and practices throughout your business is another way to stand apart. Customers increasingly expect some kind of social responsibility from the companies with which they are doing business, so incorporating such practices in your operations can only help you.

The service or product line portion of a business plan is your opportunity to outline what you offer, how you create that something, and why it meets the needs of your target market. By following the outline provided and steering clear of the common mistakes, this section of your business plan will be another piece of the puzzle that will show investors that your business is worth the risk.

Keep it exciting, and make sure you include compelling visuals. Short of a live demo or taste test, your ability to make your product or service pop off the page, or screen, is the best way to capture your readers' attention.

9

WRITING AN OPERATIONAL PLAN TO GUIDE YOUR BUSINESS

As with your business plan, your operational plan will generally be a living, breathing document. Especially in the early days of your business, you are learning so much each day that you will often be iterating on your operational plan on a daily basis as well.

A FANTASTIC OPERATIONAL PLAN FOR A BUSINESS PLAN SHOULD INCLUDE THE FOLLOWING KEY ELEMENTS.

Production plan:

Your production plan describes your company's production process, including how the product or service is manufactured or provided, the materials and equipment required, and the production schedule.

Depending on your business type, you will include the elements described above in your production plan. For example, a manufacturing business will have a much more robust production plan than a company that provides a service.

Operations process flow:

The operations process flow is a visual representation of how your company operates.

This might include the specific steps involved in producing or providing the product or service and how they fit together. In essence, this is a visual representation of the production plan that allows potential investors, and you, the business owner, to understand how everything comes together.

I've found that it is helpful to designate, using colors or different shapes, which parts of your process are internal to your company, and which parts of your process rely on outside help. Naturally, any part of the process that relies on vendors or contractors is less in your control, so understanding where the potential weak links are in your process is very important.

Supply chain management:

Irrespective of whether you manufacture or just resell products, a supply chain feeds into how you operate. Your supply chain management section is simply a description of how your company procures raw materials, components, and finished goods and how it manages inventory.

Again, depending on the size of your company, this might be something that you handle internally, or it might be something that a third-party logistics company handles on your behalf. Either way, detailing how this process works will allow you to share your vision for the business and manage the process's different components.

Quality control:

A company is only as good as what it sells. Thus, the quality control section of your business plan will describe how you manage quality throughout your production process. This includes how you ensure the quality of your products or services and identify and resolve any issues that come up during your inspections. Investors and lenders want to see that you are dedicated to providing high-quality products because this means that customers will adore your products.

Capacity and scalability:

A significant component of raising capital from outside investors is demonstrating your ability to grow and scale the company. As such, providing an analysis of your company's capacity and scalability will benefit your efforts. In this section of the report, you should include whom you plan to expand your operations without increasing your costs excessively to meet the anticipated demand for your products or services.

In reality, when your demand increases, you may or may not follow this plan exactly, but putting pen to paper around how you will approach this will be comforting to the individuals who are considering funding your business with their money.

Facilities and equipment:

Again, depending on the type of business that you are operating, this section of your business plan may be either very skinny or very robust. The facilities and equipment section of your business plan should include where your facilities and equipment are located, how the facilities are laid out, and what equipment is required to produce or provide your product or service.

This section might also include a description of the facilities and equipment of the manufacturing partners with which you are working. It is important for potential investors and yourself to understand how each component of your business operates, even if it is not operating under your own roof.

Finally, be sure to include a description of your company's maintenance and repair procedures, including how it schedules and performs routine maintenance and handles equipment breakdowns and repairs. This is especially important if your business relies on these machines to manufacture or deliver your products.

Human resources:

Human resources may be large or small in your organization; however, the people who keep your company running are very important. Use this section to describe your people strategy. For example, how do you intend to recruit, train, and retain employees, and how will you manage your workforce? The insights are key for others to understand the likelihood of your success as a business and as a leader.

Along with your human resources strategy should be a description of your health and safety policy and procedures. This should include how you ensure the safety of its employees and customers and how you comply with relevant regulations. Again, this section will be more robust in manufacturing companies and less so in IT consulting businesses.

Technology and automation:

One of the most efficient ways to scale a business is to implement technology and add automation through your processes. Use this section to describe your company's technology and automation strategy. This includes how you intend to leverage technology to improve your operations, scale your business, reduce costs, increase efficiency, and ultimately, better serve your customers.

If you think automation and AI technology will not be used in your "everyday business," then think again. Going back to our donut shop, you could use automation or AI to help you generate social media posts or develop special promotions that you can run to help drive business. There are tools out there, like ChatGPT, that allow you to ask relatively complex questions and get solid options for how to move forward.

Risk management:

Your risk management strategy will identify and assess any potential risks to your operations. This can include supply chain disruptions, potential threats to your outsource manufacturing, equipment failures, personnel issues, and more. Also included in this section should be your strategy around how you intend to mitigate these risks, or at the very least, how you will respond if an issue does arise in one or more of these areas.

Continual improvement:

The key to growth is how you evolve and improve as a company. Providing this section that describes how you plan to build continual improvement into your process is important for investors and you as a business leader. This will include how you plan to identify and implement process improvements and how you intend to track the effectiveness of those improvements.

Compliance and regulations:

Different industries will require different levels of detail when it comes to the compliance and regulation section of your business plan; however, every business plan should include some level of explanation around this topic.

This will consist of how your company complies with relevant regulations and standards, such as health and safety, environmental, and industry-specific regulations. Boring but required.

Resource allocation:

In any business, especially at the beginning, resources are finite. Including a description of how your company will allocate resources such as labor, equipment, and materials will demonstrate your ability to operate an efficient and cost-effective business. Also important here will be milestones at which you will need to either hire more employees or add more equipment to meet the demand you are experiencing.

Performance metrics:

Arguably the most important piece of any section of your business plan, performance metrics can make or break a company. Understanding the inputs and outputs of your business as well as how your actions can impact those results, will allow you to truly drive your business.

This section will include a description of the key performance metrics that you will use to measure the performance of your operations. This can consist of everything from productivity and efficiency to customer satisfaction and profit margins. Still, more importantly, you should demonstrate how you will use this data to improve your operations over time.

NOW, WE WILL DISCUSS THE TOP MISTAKES PEOPLE MAKE WHEN WRITING UP AN OPERATIONAL PLAN FOR THEIR BUSINESS.

Lack of detail

This goes for almost any section of your business plan, but one of the biggest mistakes people make when writing an operational plan is not providing enough detail. The point of an operational plan is to painstakingly detail every aspect of the business.

This is not just for potential investors but also for you, as the business owner, to fully understand where the risks lie in your approach to the business.

This will include everything that we discussed above. Still, the main point here is that excluding this information will lead to questions from outside investors as to how your plan to produce your products, provide your service, and ultimately make money in your business.

Lack of focus on scalability:

Another common mistake is not considering scalability or, put plainly, not considering how you intend to grow your business. In most cases, you are putting together a business plan to raise capital from outside investors.

Outside investors are interested in your business and what you do, but they are most interested in what kind of return they can get on their investment. This means that it is your job to plan for and demonstrate how the company plans to expand its operations, increase the demand for your products or services, and meet that increased demand. This information is necessary for potential investors to understand how the business will grow long-term and what it means for them.

This scalability plan should include your approach to integrating technology and automation into your processes. Technology and automation are the number one ways to increase your efficiency without adding headcount to your business, which means that you will be able to scale your business without adding a lot of expenses.

Not considering risks or compliance and regulations:

There are risks associated with absolutely every kind of business. Whether you're a mom-and-pop hardware store or a global conglomerate, there will be risks in what you are doing. The worst thing that you can do as a business owner is not considering these potential risks and not plan for how to mitigate these risks.

Along the same lines, considering how your company will comply with relevant regulations and standards will put you in a good position. Unfortunately, regulations impact every business out there, so crafting your approach around these will only help you succeed. You cannot ignore these.

Not providing performance metrics:

Key performance metrics are, for lack of a better word, the key to how you will operate your business. Demonstrating your ability to focus on the metrics that matter in terms of the performance of your operations is important for any potential investor to see.

Additionally, having a continuous improvement plan for how you identify weak areas of your business plan and how you will measure the effectiveness of any changes you make is required if you intend to succeed.

Not including enough visual aids

When writing your operational plan, the final thing to avoid is not including enough visual aids to demonstrate how you operate your business. This will consist of things like flowcharts, diagrams, and images.

These items will clearly show how your operations are set up and will be more engaging and memorable for potential investors and other readers of your operational plan. Ultimately, this is your playbook for running your business, so it would behoove you to make it as easy to understand as possible.

NEXT, HERE IS HOW YOU CAN SET YOURSELF APART WITH A SOLID, ENGAGING OPERATIONAL PLAN.

Include a technology strategy:

Many smaller businesses fail to utilize technology to the fullest. At the very least, you should envision how technology can improve your business in the future, even if it is not something you can implement today.

Including a technology strategy in your operational plan will show that you are forward-thinking and committed to using technology to improve your operations, reduce your costs, and improve your efficiency as a business.

This could include using different forms of automation, artificial intelligence, data analytics, or other industry-specific ways of streamlining your operations and performance as a company. Including this advanced thought will also impress upon potential investors that you are thinking big about your business.

Outline a sustainability plan:

Sustainability in life and business is becoming more important by the day.

Demonstrating your company's commitment to environmental and social responsibility is one way to differentiate yourself from others in your industry. It might also already be a standard part of the industry in which you operate, so not including this could be a big miss on your part.

Include customer service strategy:

Irrespective of the type of business that you are in, customer service is king. For example, you might be servicing consumers directly, or you might be providing a product or service to another company. In either case, providing excellent customer service is strategically very important for your business. Including details around that strategy in your operational plan will genuinely demonstrate your company's commitment to providing a high level of service to its customers, which can be a differentiating factor.

Include performance measurement system:

We've focused a lot on performance metrics, but one way to differentiate your business is to outline how you will measure your performance. It is one thing to say that you focus on specific metrics, but including a screenshot of a dashboard that you use to operate your business and spot potential issues in your business will set you apart as a business owner.

Making it simple to track and monitor performance is important for you and anyone looking to invest in your business. This will demonstrate your company's commitment, and your commitment personally, to growing and improving your business. It will also ensure that everyone involved clearly understands how the company will measure its success.

Include a disaster recovery and continuity plan:

You've detailed the risks and risk mitigation strategies that you will use, so taking it a step further by including a disaster recovery and continuity plan in the operational plan can help to hammer home the fact that you are building this business for long-term success.

Demonstrating that you have thought through how to maintain a continuity of operations in the event of unexpected disruptions, such as natural disasters, power outages, or equipment failures, will certainly put you a level above others in your industry. This will also help build confidence with potential investors and lenders that you have thought through every minute detail to minimize disruptions to its operations and keep the business running.

Use case studies or examples:

If you are just starting your business, then using case studies or examples from similar companies or industries can demonstrate the effectiveness of the company's operational strategies and plans. Specifically, you can outline how you bring a business model from a different industry and apply it to your industry. You may also point to failures in other business models and how your model solves these. Ultimately, saying to investors that you will be the "Uber of [insert industry here]" will, at the very least, be both engaging and memorable for anyone reading your business plan.

Your operational plan is intended to demonstrate your commitment and ability to run a well-functioning business. Taking the extra steps to add as much detail as possible to this portion of your business plan will benefit you by helping you understand your business fully and demonstrating the same to potential investors. Use this operational plan to help guide you as a business owner, and iterate on this plan often. Remember, your entire business plan, and this operational plan in particular, is a living document that is intended to evolve as your business grows.

10

BUILDING A FINANCIAL PLAN THAT WILL ALLOW YOUR BUSINESS TO SUCCEED

A financial plan is a crucial part of any business plan, and we'll detail the different components in this next chapter. Contrary to popular belief, creating such a plan without an accounting background is possible, so don't feel stressed if you don't feel like this is your strong suit.

Ahead of that, though, I think it is important to walk you through the different ways to fund your business. How you're funded will dictate how you set up your financial model in a few ways, so reviewing these methods before diving into the financial modeling portion of the business plan is prudent.

We will review this in order of least costly from an ownership perspective to most expensive. By this, I mean as we progress through the different funding types, you will effectively give away more equity in your business to secure the capital required to start or grow your business. Consequently, this is also ordered in my preferred funding method for a new venture.

BOOTSTRAPPING

If you have the capital to go this route comfortably, I would highly suggest it for at least the first few months of operations.

Bootstrapping a business refers to the process of starting and growing your new business without taking on external funding. Essentially, instead of relying on investors or loans, you use your personal capital to fund the business until you become profitable. Keep in mind if you bootstrap your business at the beginning, you can always take on external investments later.

The benefit of doing this is that you have time to validate your business plan before an outside investor puts a valuation on the company. If you have some revenue and traction, you will receive a higher valuation for your company. Therefore you will receive more money while keeping a greater percentage of the business.

This method requires a strong individual. You must be resourceful, creative, and very frugal in managing business expenses. This might look like using low-cost or free marketing strategies or operating with a very small team as you get things up and running.

As mentioned, the main advantage of bootstrapping is that you get to retain full ownership and full control of your business. External investors bring capital, but they also bring pressure and obligations that you need to consider as you operate your business.

As a business owner, this method also forces you to focus on creating a profitable business with profitable unit economics from day one. So it's very clear that you become much more creative about surviving when you have skin in the game.

The drawback to bootstrapping, though, is that you need to have incredible wealth to be able to grow the business quickly. You will not be able to invest in expensive advertising or hire large teams, and you may not be able to compete with others with a large amount of funding. Additionally, you will sometimes be forced to choose between growth, profitability, and survival. And there will likely be times when you need to reinvest revenue into your business rather than taking a salary.

GRANTS

If you're able to find a grant that is suitable for your business, then apply as soon as possible. Grants are an excellent type of funding because grants do not have to be repaid, and you do not have to give up ownership in your company to accept a grant.

Typically, grants are awarded by government agencies, non-profit organizations, and foundations. These types of grants, though, often have very specific eligibility criteria.

Business grants can be used for everything from start-up costs, research and development expenses, and expansion initiatives. When you are awarded and accept a grant, you must put the money received towards the intended purpose within your business.

Some examples of business grants include:

- Small Business Innovation Research (SBIR) and Small Business Technology Transfer (STTR) grants:

    These are federal grants that are awarded to small businesses for research and development in specific technology areas. There are very specific criteria for each of these grants, which are very difficult to secure.

- State and local economic development grants:

Many states and local governments offer grants to businesses that are looking to expand or relocate to their area. However, you're more likely to qualify for these grants, so if you find a grant that applies to your business, be sure to apply for that grant!

- Industry-specific grants:

Some grants are specific to certain industries, such as grants for renewable energy or grants for women-owned businesses. Again, these are difficult to come by, but worth the effort if you do find a grant that applies to your business.

Applying for grants will require much of what you've prepared by creating your business plan. You will typically need to submit a proposal that outlines your specific project or your business as a whole, but this depends on the grant type for which you are applying.

The application process for any grant is very competitive. However, before spending time filling out hundreds of applications, be sure to take the time to research each grant to understand whether your business or project fits within the guidelines of the grant itself.

Because grants are non-dilutive and do not need to be repaid, they are a wonderful funding source. However, they are quite hard to come by and can have some very specific hoops through which you will need to jump to even be considered for the funds.

LOANS

Business loans are a very common type of debt financing where a lender, typically a bank, provides a business with a sum of money that must be repaid with interest over an agreed-upon period of time. While banks are the most common source, loans can come from other sources, including credit unions and online lenders that are not banks.

The challenge with business loans when starting your business is that the terms will not be in your favor, and, in some cases, banks will only loan you money if you have a minimum of two years of business history. However, the terms of a business loan can vary depending on many factors, including, who the lender is, the type of loan, and the borrower's credit score.

Here are a few of the more common types of business loans:

- Term loans:
- These are traditional loans with a fixed interest rate, a set repayment period, and a fixed monthly payment. Similar to a mortgage you might take out on a house, this is a very common loan structure.
- Line of credit:
- This type of loan allows a business to borrow up to a certain limit as needed and pay interest only on the amount borrowed. Often, this type of loan requires collateral against which you need to borrow. If you have a line of credit against your home, for example, you're leveraging personal assets to secure the loan. This can get dangerous.
- Invoice financing:
- This type of loan allows a business to borrow against its outstanding invoices.
- This is also called Accounts Receivable financing and is a great way to help in scenarios when cash flow is an issue.
- However, this requires you to have a business that is already in operation.
- Equipment financing:

- This type of loan is used to purchase equipment or machinery for a business.

In this case, you're leveraging the value of the equipment to secure the capital to purchase that equipment. You might compare this type of loan to a car loan.

As mentioned, the main challenge with applying for business loans, specifically when you are just getting your business started, is that the amount of money you can borrow depends on you as an individual. The bank will look to you to provide collateral for the loan if something doesn't work out for your business. For this type of funding, your personal creditworthiness is the deciding factor on whether you're able to secure the loan.

On the other hand, securing a loan for a business that has an operating history requires a different set of requirements. The financial institution will look at the business's financial health, including revenue, cash flow, and profitability. As a business owner applying for loans, you must bring a strong business plan and clear, realistic financial projections to apply for the loan.

As noted above, business loans require a personal guarantee, meaning that if the business cannot pay the loan, the lender will go after the business owner's personal assets. This is inherently risky, so it makes sense to apply for such loans once you have some traction in the business.

Compared to equity investment, which we will review next, business loans must be paid back with interest, and the business does not relinquish ownership in the process. This makes it a good option for businesses that either have some traction and revenue or have a clear plan for how they will use the funds and can repay the loan over time.

EQUITY INVESTMENTS

The last type of funding source that we will cover is an equity investment. This refers to when a business raises capital by selling ownership in the company. This usually happens in the form of stock, which means that the investors, or the firms injecting capital into a business, become shareholders.

As shareholders, these investors have a say in how the business operates and rights to the profits and assets of the company. Specifically, in exchange for their money, shareholders have a right to profits through dividends. They have the opportunity to see significant returns in value on their shares if the company performs well. Think of it this way; the investors are taking a risk by injecting capital into an early-stage company, and for that, they have a large potential reward at the end of the journey if the company does well.

Equity investments can come from a range of different sources, including friends, family, angel investors, venture capitalists, and private equity firms. These investors typically invest in certain types of companies.

For example, if a particular venture capital firm is focused on sustainability, then its investments will likely be made in companies that are focused on sustainable products or services. Equity investors are also looking for high-growth companies or companies that they believe have the opportunity to become very large because this is how they get paid back for the risk they are taking by investing. Finally, these investors often bring more than capital; they look for investments where they can contribute by bringing either industry connections or expertise.

The benefit of equity investments is that these investors do not expect to be paid back in the same way that debt holders expect to be paid back. Instead, these investors think much longer term and are looking for a return on their investment in the form of dividends or the sale of the company.

Now that we've covered the various types of funding sources, we'll go through the typical sections required in your financial plan for your business:

FINANCIAL PROJECTIONS

Detailed financial projections are imperative to running a successful business.

This section should include the "big three" financial statements: income statement, balance sheet, and cash flow statement. As part of this, you must include assumptions about how you expect to achieve the projected financial results. These assumptions will fuel the key financial metrics in your projections, including revenue, margin, and net income.

If you are just starting your business, creating financial projections can be challenging, but it is an important step in developing a solid business plan. If you're starting a fresh business, here are some steps to help you create financial projections for your business that has no history:

Start by gathering data:

First, collect as much data as possible about your market, industry, and competitors. You have done a lot of this work for previous sections of your business plan, so this shouldn't be too tall of a task. This data will help you to make realistic assumptions about the size of the market, the demand for your product or service, and the pricing and costs you can expect to incur.

Solid financial projections are only as good as the data behind the assumptions that created those projections. Additionally, any astute investor will dig into your assumptions, so having the data to back up your numbers is extremely important.

Develop a sales forecast:

Using the data that you have collected, you will want to create a sales forecast that outlines your projected revenue and sales growth over the next several years. It is very important that this forecast be based on the research that you have done and that this forecast takes into account the size of your addressable market, the demand for your product, and the strategy by which you intend to generate these kinds of sales numbers.

Create an income statement:

Now, you will create an income statement that shows your key metrics, including your projected revenue, cost of goods sold, gross margin, operating expenses, and net income. This statement should include both projected and historical data, if available. This is one of the "big three" financial statements that are important for any business.

There are a number of templates that you can find online for a financial model. I've included a link to a model that I've used previously as well:

Link to the financial model template: https://linktr.ee/kaycarroll

Create a balance sheet:

Using your income statement, you will now create a balance sheet that shows your projected assets, liabilities, and equity over the next several years. This statement should include both projected and historical data, if available.

Don't worry if you feel like you're creating these statements out of thin air because, in many ways, you are!

Your financial projections, and the associated financial model, are your best guess as to what your business will do, and they are rooted in the educated assumptions that you are making.

Create a cash flow statement:

Finally, you will use your income statement and balance sheet to create a cash flow statement that shows your projected cash flow from operating activities, investing activities, and financing activities.

Include assumptions and risks:

In your financial model, it is important to explain all of the thinking that you have put into each section. Specifically, you must explain how you arrived at your assumptions and the risks that are inherent in the assumptions that power your financial model. To create this model, you used many assumptions, including market size, assumptions behind sales numbers, pricing, and costs.

These numbers were not created purely by guessing, and if they were, then you need to go back and reevaluate your assumptions. These were created by researching your market and making educated decisions about what you expect to happen. That said, offering an explanation for how you arrived at these numbers will be key to getting investors on board.

Get your projections reviewed:

When you are engulfed in a project, it becomes difficult to check your own work.

As such, it is important to have someone with a financial background read through your model to ensure that you are providing accurate and realistic projections for both yourself and your potential investors.

Update your projections:

You are learning more about your business each and every day. As you learn, your business will evolve, and as your business evolves, you should update your projections to reflect the reality of how you have performed. Additionally, as and when different elements of the market change, be sure to update your forward-looking projections to account for such changes.

Creating accurate financial projections is an iterative process, and it may take many weeks or months to get your numbers right. Revisiting your model and your projections often will help you to build a thriving business as you incorporate your daily learnings into the assumptions that you are making.

Break-Even Analysis:

Another prudent thing for you to do is to run a break-even analysis on your business.

Investors and lenders are interested in how they will be paid back on the investment or loan that they are providing to a business. A break-even analysis shows the point in time at which the business will start to make a profit. Your analysis should include a detailed calculation of the fixed and variable costs and the revenue required to cover those costs.

Keep in mind that your analysis is based on a number of different assumptions around sales, costs, and a host of other things. Like your financial model, this analysis should be a living document that you regularly revisit in order to incorporate what you've learned about your business.

Because this is such an important tool for your business, we've outlined the steps you can take to run a break-even analysis for your business:

Determine fixed and variable costs:

First, determine all of the costs that your business will incur and divide them into fixed costs and variable costs. Fixed costs are expenses that do not change regardless of the level of production or sales.

These are things like rent and salaries that will stay the same irrespective of your sales. Variable costs are expenses that change based on the level of production or sales. These are things like the cost of goods sold, shipping expenses, and sales commissions.

Calculate the total fixed costs & variable costs:

Add all of the fixed costs that you identified in the first step to calculate your total fixed costs. Next, add all of the variable costs that you identified to calculate your total variable costs.

Determine the unit price and unit variable cost:

Now, divide the total fixed costs by the number of units that you anticipate selling. This will give you the unit cost, which is the absolute minimum price that you need to charge for each unit in order to cover your fixed costs.

Next, divide the total variable costs by the number of units you anticipate selling. This is your variable unit cost. Add this to your fixed unit cost to get the total unit cost, which is the cost of each unit.

Calculate the break-even point:

Finally, to determine the break-even point, divide the total fixed costs by the difference between the unit price and the unit variable cost. This will give you the number of units you need to sell in order to cover your fixed costs and start to make a profit.

Use the break-even point to create a projection:

You can now use the break-even point to create a projection that shows when the business will start to make a profit and how much profit it will make. When you will break even is a question that will be asked of you, often, as you are speaking with investors and vendors about your business.

Sensitivity analysis:

Because so much of what you are projecting in your financial model and in your break-even analysis is based on assumption, it is also important to consider what happens if things don't go as planned. What happens to the break-even point if costs are higher or if sales are lower? This is known as a sensitivity analysis, and it will allow you to understand how changes in costs or sales affect the break-even point of your business.

With this break-even analysis, you'll continue to prove to your potential investors or lenders that you have really thought through your business plan. This is yet another exercise in building trust before bringing on partners in your business.

CAPITAL REQUIREMENTS

Another important section of your financial plan is the section that details your capital requirements. Put simply; this section is a detailed analysis of how much money you need for start-up costs, working capital, and any additional money that you need to help support the growth of the business before you reach your break-even point.

Start-up costs:

Start-up costs are everything that you need to get yourself into business. When estimating the start-up costs for your business, it's important to include the following items:

Equipment and inventory:

You must think about the equipment, tools, or inventory that you will need on day one in order to operate your business.

Office expenses:

Will you need to rent an office or retail space? What will the utilities cost for this space? These are the questions that you must answer in your office expense section.

Legal and professional fees:

Often times you will need an entity through which to operate your business. In order to set up an LLC, for example, you will need to spend money upfront on legal services. Additionally, it might be wise to enlist the help of an accountant to set up your books and review your financial projections.

Insurance:

Depending on the business that you are operating, you may need liability insurance, worker's compensation insurance, automobile insurance, or property insurance. This is all completely dictated by your type of business.

Marketing and advertising:

In order to drive business, you will likely need to spend money on marketing and advertising. This could include the cost associated with creating a website, developing advertisements, or promoting your business via online advertising.

Salaries and wages:

Again, depending on the business that you are in, you may need to hire others to help you on day one. In order to get people to help you, you will need to pay them. In your start-up costs, it is important to include the cost of paying yourself and any employees you plan to hire.

Travel and miscellaneous expenses:

You may or may not need to travel in order to sell your product.

Budgeting for such expenses that are not included in other categories is important. Be sure to include expenses such as travel expenses, business licenses, and permits.

Reserve funds:

Think of your reserve funds as a safety net. If not everything goes according to your well-crafted plan, then you will want to budget for some reserve funds to cover any unforeseen expenses.

As noted throughout this book, the cost of starting a business can vary widely depending on the type of business and location. You will need to research and speak to experts in your field to truly understand the realistic costs for you to get your business up and running.

Additionally, you must have a clear understanding of your business model and how it will generate revenue to ensure the financial sustainability of your business.

Working capital:

Working capital is the amount of money that you need for your business in order to cover your day-to-day operational expenses. This includes paying your employees, paying bills, purchasing inventory, and anything else required to keep your business operating.

Working capital is essential to any business as it allows the business to cover its short-term expenses and obligations while waiting for revenue to hit the bank account. This is especially important when starting a business, as you need to ensure that you have enough money to cover your expenses while you're building the business.

To plan for your working capital requirements, follow these steps:

Estimate your start-up costs:

Use the start-up cost estimate that you put together previously.

With this, you will have a clear understanding of the costs associated with starting your business, including equipment, inventory, and office expenses. This will give you an idea of how much money you'll need to get the business up and running.

Project your cash flow:

Next, develop a cash flow projection that shows when and how much money you expect to come in and when and how much you expect to go out. You should create different scenarios where revenue takes longer to come in as a way of protecting yourself from unknowns. This cash flow model will help you identify any potential shortfalls in working capital.

Identify sources of financing:

Determine how you will cover your start-up costs. We outlined the different sources of funding previously, so this is your moment to select from those sources for your funding.

Establish credit:

Building relationships with suppliers and vendors is always important and is especially important when you're starting out. By cultivating relationships, you may be able to negotiate more favorable payment terms, or even financing options, directly with your suppliers. You're really looking for someone to take a chance on you!

Keep a buffer:

As mentioned in the cash flow section above, create scenarios where you do not meet your revenue expectations. From this, you will be able to carve out a buffer of working capital to keep on hand in the event of slow sales periods or changes that are outside of your control.

Monitor and review:

As with nearly every portion of your financial plan and your business plan, this is an iterative process. Review your cash flow projections and financial performance regularly so that you are able to make adjustments as needed.

Having enough working capital is the difference between companies that thrive and companies that go out of business.

Sometimes, being able to survive, especially in the early years, is the most important thing that you can do.

CASH IS KING.

Other funding to support growth

While start-up costs and working capital are the most common types of funding required when a business is just opening up, there are other types of funding that businesses may need in order to start or grow their operations.

Expansion capital:

The name says it all! As a business grows, that business may need funding in order to grow its operations. This could be in the form of hiring additional employees, purchasing new machinery, or opening a new location.

Research and development:

Businesses that rely on the development or improvement of technology may require funding for research and development purposes. This type of capital allows businesses to create new products or improve existing products that they have already developed.

Inventory:

For businesses that stock and sell inventory, inventory financing might be required. Because of the nature of business, it is sometimes required to purchase inventory upfront in order to sell that inventory. Oftentimes, there is a gap between when businesses must pay for the inventory and when businesses will be paid for the sale of that same inventory. In these cases, inventory financing is available to help bridge the gap.

Marketing and advertising:

If a business has a product or service that works but lacks funds to advertise or market the business, then it may need funding to promote its products and services and attract new customers. In these situations, a strong financial model and relevant case studies will make raising funds much easier.

Mergers and acquisitions:

We've talked a lot about organic business growth, but another way to grow is via acquisitions. There may be times when the best course of action for growth or to fill a technology gap in the business is to merge with or acquire another company. The result of this is an expansion of operations in some cases, and in other cases, it might be growth in customers.

Real estate:

Finally, businesses may need funding to purchase or lease commercial real estate. In these cases, it is important for the business to evaluate the purpose of the expense and ensure that it fits into the growth of the business.

In general, the type of funding that a business needs will depend on the circumstances of the business as well as what that business is looking to achieve. Some businesses may require specialized forms of funding, while others can start, operate, and grow by tapping into a loan.

Be sure to consider the purpose of the capital and be thoughtful about where that money is coming from.

Not all capital is created equal.

SENSITIVITY ANALYSIS

Next in your financial planning portion of your business plan should be a sensitivity analysis of your financial projections. This section shows how your projection will change under different scenarios.

For example, if revenue is half of what you were projecting, then will your business survive? This exercise is very useful to help identify both opportunities and risks for businesses. This will also help investors and lenders get comfortable with the assumptions that you are making and the risks that you are taking.

We discussed sensitivity analysis briefly earlier in the section, but we'll expand on this exercise here. Put simply, a sensitivity analysis is a tool that helps businesses understand how changes in key assumptions, such as revenue, costs, and interest rates, will affect their financial projections.

The key things to consider when performing a sensitivity analysis include the following:

Key variables:

Identifying and understanding the variables that have the greatest impact on your financial projections, such as revenue, costs, and interest rates.

Scenarios:

Using your knowledge of the business environment, develop a range of scenarios that reflect different potential outcomes for the key variables that you have identified. For example, you might consider a best-case scenario, a most likely scenario, and a worst-case scenario.

Impact on financial projections:

For each scenario, calculate the impact on your financial projections, such as net income, cash flow, and return on investment.

Break-even point:

Identify the point at which your business will break even, which is the point at which revenue equals costs.

Sensitivity range:

Determine the range of values for each variable that would still allow the business to achieve its objectives.

Risk assessment:

Assess the level of risk associated with each scenario and consider how the business can mitigate those risks.

Summarize the results of the sensitivity analysis and make recommendations for how the business can respond to the different scenarios.

This analysis will allow you to better understand the potential risks and opportunities associated with your financial projections and ultimately help you to make more informed decisions about how to allocate resources and manage risk.

EXIT STRATEGY

While not all owners intend to exit their businesses, at some point, this will likely be the case. This section includes information on the exit strategy for the business, such as an initial public offering (IPO), sale to a strategic buyer, or a management buyout.

This will help potential investors understand your strategy as well as what their timeline is to see a return on their investment. As such, whichever exit strategy you cover should also include a detailed analysis of the potential return on investment for investors.

We will run through a few of the exit options that you might consider.

Selling a business to a strategic or individual buyer

This is a process in which a business is sold to another company, or individual, that operates in the same industry or market. The buyer may also be a company or individual that does not operate in the same industry but would like to enter that industry.

Typically, the buyer is looking to acquire the business for strategic reasons, including gaining access to new customers, products, or technology, and will use this acquisition to expand their current operations. In other cases, the buyer is interested in gaining a footprint in a completely new market, and the most efficient way to do this is through acquisition.

Here is a general overview of how the process works. We'll highlight specifically what might be useful to include in the exit strategy portion of your business plan:

Identifying potential buyers:

Investors will be curious about what it is that you are building towards and how you intend to achieve that kind of exit. When considering strategic buyers for your business, you will want to identify potential buyers that are a good fit for the business. These buyers may include competitors, suppliers, customers, or other companies in the same industry.

Imagining the deal:

For inventors, you will want to provide a theory around what the potential terms of the sale with the buyer might look like. This may include an estimate of the purchase price, payment structure, and what the impact of those estimates will be for potential investors.

For sellers and for their investors, selling your business to a strategic buyer can be more financially beneficial for you because the buyer may be able to pay a higher price than a financial buyer, as they see the strategic value in the business.

Additionally, a strategic buyer may be able to help the business to grow and expand in ways that you may not have been able to achieve on your own. When considering seller financing, you might be able to capitalize on this growth through the terms of your seller financing.

If selling to a strategic buyer is in your plans, then it is important to have a good understanding of the market, the industry, and the legal and regulatory requirements involved in the process of selling your business to a strategic buyer before you get started with building your business.

Management buyout (MBO):

A management buyout is a process in which a business is acquired by its current management team rather than by an outside buyer. If you have strong partners in your business, but you are the sole legal owner of the company, then a management buyout could be a way for you to cash out on a portion of your business while adding great strategic value by allowing your partners to become owners in the business.

Here is a general overview of how the process works:

Identifying the opportunity:

In general, the management team that is heavily involved in the day-to-day operations of the business will be able to identify the opportunity to buy the business. This could be because the owner is interested in selling or because they believe that the business would be more successful under a different ownership structure.

Putting together a proposal:

The management team then would put together a proposal outlining the details of the buyout. This includes the proposed purchase price, the financing structure, and the strategy that the management team intends to deploy within the business after the buyout.

Securing financing:

Next, the management team would need to secure financing to complete the buyout. This may involve obtaining a business loan, raising equity from investors, or a combination of both. This may also include seller financing, especially if the management team is on good terms with you, the seller.

Due Diligence:

Before closing the deal, the management team and the current owner will conduct due diligence on the business, which includes reviewing the financial and operational information of the business and the legal documents. This process typically takes a couple of months to complete as each party, specifically, the purchasing party, will go through each minor detail of the business that they intend to purchase.

Closing the deal:

Once all the parties are satisfied with the terms of the sale, the deal will be closed, and the management team will become the new owners of the business.

Integrating the changes:

After the closing, the management team will need to integrate the changes and implement their plans for the business.

Because the management team already has a deep understanding of the business and the day-to-day operations of the business, a management buyout can be beneficial for the seller and lead to a very smooth transition.

This type of buyout allows the current management team to step up and take control of the business, ultimately making decisions that they believe will make the business more successful. It's important to have a well-thought-out plan and to secure financing before attempting a management buyout, as well as a solid understanding of the legal and regulatory requirements involved in the process.

Initial public offering (IPO)

An initial public offering is a process by which a private company becomes a publicly traded company by issuing shares of stock to the public. This is typically reserved for very large corporations, so we won't go into too much detail here.

Before going public, the company will typically hire an investment bank to act as the underwriter of the offering. The investment bank will help the company with the preparation of the registration statement and prospectus, which will be filed with the Securities and Exchange Commission (SEC). The company will also need to prepare for the increased regulatory and financial reporting requirements that come with being a public company.

The company will embark on a "roadshow" to meet with potential investors, including institutional investors and high-net-worth individuals, to generate interest in the offering. This is an opportunity for the company to present its business plan, its financial performance and prospects, and the management team to potential investors.

The investment bank will work with the company to determine the offering price for the stock. The price is typically set through a process known as "book building," in which the investment bank solicits bids from potential investors to determine the demand for the stock.

Once the offering price has been determined, the shares are allotted to investors, and the stock begins trading on a stock exchange.

After the IPO, the company becomes a publicly traded company and must comply with the regulatory and financial reporting requirements of being a public company. The company will also be subject to increased scrutiny from investors, analysts, and the media.

An IPO is a very significant event in the life of a business. It can bring a large amount of capital and allow investors to liquidate their stake in the company, but it also comes with a host of regulatory and financial reporting requirements, as well as increased scrutiny from investors and the public. Not all companies are meant to reach this kind of exit, and in fact, only 1% of all companies go through an initial public offering each year in the United States.

To wrap up, a financial plan should be comprehensive and realistic and provide a clear understanding of the company's financial position, funding requirements, and exit strategy. It should also be presented in a clear and easy-to-understand format, with enough supporting documents and analysis to back up the financial projections.

CONCLUSION

Whatever your business future holds, one thing is for certain. By going through the process of writing a proper business plan, detailing your approach to the business, and really thinking through what you are attempting to you, you will be better prepared than 95% of entrepreneurs out there. This book guided you through the process of writing a comprehensive business plan. Now it is your job to execute that plan, iterate, and execute again.

Your goal with this business plan is not only to flesh out your business and get a handle on how you will achieve your goals but also to show the reader of the business plan that you are the right person to bring your vision to life.

You must prove that you are an expert.

While it might seem unimportant to think through the minute details of a business plan when you are at the idea stage, it is important that you go through this process. Start with a solid executive summary that highlights the key elements of your business plan and hooks the reader. As mentioned, your executive summary is potentially the only thing that someone reads before deciding whether or not to entertain your proposal.

As such, you need to make your business shine in this first section.

Next, you'll go into the details behind what you presented in that executive summary.

Your company description should share the general details of your business as well as any history of how you got started. Additionally, this is the time for you to share your mission statement and, ultimately, to share the purpose behind what it is that you are building.

Essentially, use this section to create a connection between the reader, potential investors and lenders, and the mission of your company. While this is a business plan, one of the best ways to get people interested is by connecting with them emotionally.

After sharing more about the purpose of your company, you'll help the reader understand how your business fits within the industry and within your specific market.

Remember, you are an expert in your particular business, and this is your time to demonstrate that. Educate the reader on industry trends and how you are taking advantage of the trends that you see. Help the reader to understand a gap that you see in the market.

After painting the picture of the industry and the market, you will take readers through the current players in the game - your competitors. You will analyze the approaches of your competitors and show that you are learning from what they are doing well while correcting for mistakes that they are making. Be sure to give your competitors credit where credit is due and take those learnings into your own business.

Next, present to your readers how your business is poised to take advantage of the gap that you previously identified in the market. You need to take readers through your sales and marketing plan, show off the product or service that you are bringing to market (including visuals!), and get into the nitty-gritty of how you intend to make all of this happen.

You've now effectively shown the audience what you are building and how you are going to make it a success, so the last question to answer for them is how you will provide a return on your investment. This is where the financial plan comes into the picture. A detailed, well-thought-out financial plan, as we described, will be the icing on the cake when it comes to securing the future of your business.

Sounds easy, right? It's not easy, but it is important to go through this process, and a solid business plan will pay dividends for years to come.

At the beginning of your business, this plan will be how you secure funding for your new venture and how you will continue to attract investors along the way.

It will be the roadmap for the growth of your business and the ultimate success of your business.

Take your time and revisit each of the chapters as you craft the different sections of your business plan. There are dos and don't in each section that will help you to avoid big mistakes and will set you up for success.

Apply these lessons as you craft your business plan, and most importantly, treat this as a living, breathing document. Revisit your business plan often, especially in the early days, and apply the learnings that you are gathering in the day-to-day operation of the business.

And remember - you've got this. Now is the time to get started. You have all of the tools necessary to build a thriving business, and you just have to take the plunge!

REFERENCES

How to Write the Business Plan Products and Services Section. https://www.thebalancemoney.com/business-plan-format-1794224

Purpose of Writing Business Plan: Effective Guide - INK. https://inkforall.com/ai-writing-tools/write-business-plans/purpose-of-writing-a-business-plan/

Write a Business Plan. https://www.linkedin.com/pulse/write-business-plan-baljinder-singh

9 Indispensable Factors to Consider Before Starting a Business. https://www.litmusbranding.com/blog/indispensable-factors-to-consider-before-starting-a-business/

Feenstra, Daniela. "The Standout Business Plan: Make Irresistible- and Get the Funds You Need for Your Start-up or Growing Business." Journal of Applied Management and Entrepreneurship, vol. 19, no. 4, Greenleaf Publishing, Oct. 2014, p. 116.

Use Your Business Structure to Limit Liability | Wolters Kluwer. https://www.wolterskluwer.com/en/expert-insights/use-your-business-structure-to-limit-liability

How to write a mission statement: Guide with examples | QuickBooks. https://quickbooks.intuit.com/r/starting-a-business/how-to-write-a-mission-statement/

Calculate the start-up costs of your business | business.gov.au. https://business.gov.au/Planning/New-businesses/Calculate-the-start-up-costs-of-your-business

SWOT Analysis: A Comprehensive Guide for Businesses. https://echovalleymedia.com/swot-analysis-a-comprehensive-guide-for-businesses/

How Porter's Five Forces Help in E-commerce Business Analysis?. https://www.anscommerce.com/blog/how-porters-five-forces-help-in-e-commerce-business-analysis/

Threat Of New Entrants | Porter's Five Forces Model | Cleverism. https://www.cleverism.com/threat-of-new-entrants-porters-five-forces-model/

Gillespie, Peter. "Becoming a Real Business Partner." Accountancy Ireland, vol. 49, no. 2, Institute of Chartered Accountants In Ireland, Apr. 2017, p. 87.

Do You Know How Your Business Is Doing and Where It's Going?. https://articles.bplans.com/do-you-know-how-your-business-is-doing-and-where-its-going/

How to Start a Business in Indiana | Chamber of Commerce. https://www.chamberofcommerce.org/how-to-start-a-business-in-indiana

12 Steps to Create a Successful LinkedIn Marketing Strategy in 2023. https://shanebarker.com/blog/linkedin-marketing-strategy/

How to Write an Informal Business Report? Best Report ... - Databox. https://databox.com/informal-business-report

Small Business Grants In Michigan - Upmetrics. https://upmetrics.co/blog/small-business-grants-michigan

What Is a Financial Statement? | Detailed Overview of Main Statements. https://www.patriotsoftware.com/blog/accounting/what-is-a-financial-statement/

How to Calculate Break Even Price? 2023 - Ablison. https://www.ablison.com/how-to-calculate-break-even-price/

Direct vs. Indirect Costs | Breakdown, Examples, & Why it Matters. https://www.patriotsoftware.com/blog/accounting/direct-vs-indirect-costs-difference/

How Do You Calculate Working Capital? - Investopedia. https://www.investopedia.com/ask/answers/071114/how-do-you-calculate-working-capital.asp